Right-Minded Teamwork

9 Right Choices for Building a Team That Works as One

Do No Harm.
Work As One.®

By
Dan Hogan
Certified Master Facilitator

Books by Dan Hogan

Reason, Ego, & the Right-Minded Teamwork Myth: The Philosophy and Process for Creating a Right-Minded Team That Works Together as One

Right-Minded Teamwork in Any Team: The Ultimate Team Building Method to Create a Team That Works as One

How to Facilitate Team Work Agreements: A Practical, 10-Step Process for Building a Right-Minded Team That Works as One

How to Apply the Right Choice Model:
Create a Right-Minded Team That Works as One

7 Mindfulness Training Lessons: Improve Teammates' Ability to Work as One with Right-Minded Thinking

Right-Minded Teamwork:
9 Right Choices for Building a Team That Works as One

Design a Right-Minded, Team-Building Workshop:
12 Steps to Create a Team That Works as One

Achieve Your Organization's Strategic Plan: Create a Right-Minded Team Management System to Ensure All Teams Work as One

Copyright © 2013, 2021, 2025 by Dan Hogan, Lord & Hogan LLC.
All rights reserved.

Contact Dan Hogan at Dan.Hogan@RightMindedTeamwork.com

This book is licensed for personal, non-commercial use only. No part of this publication may be reproduced, distributed, or transmitted in any form or by any means, including photocopying, recording, or other electronic or mechanical methods, without the prior written permission of the publisher, except for brief quotations embodied in critical reviews and certain other noncommercial uses permitted by copyright law.

ISBN: 978-1-939585-07-3

Acknowledgments & Appreciations

To the thousands of teammates, team leaders, and team-building facilitators with whom I've worked with over the last 40 years,

Thank You

For being my teacher.

Collectively, we created this awesome team-building program.

Right-Minded Teamwork is a business-oriented, psychological approach to team building where acceptance, forgiveness, and adjustment are teammate characteristics, and customer satisfaction is the team's result.

In addition, there are several special people I want to joyfully acknowledge and thank for their contributions.

First and foremost, I want to convey my deep and heartfelt gratitude to our editor, Erin Leigh. Thanks to her superb editing and vital guidance, Right-Minded Teamwork is now much easier to understand and successfully integrate into your team. Thank you, Erin. The RMT book series would not have happened without you.
(To contact Erin, email erin@thechoice.life.)

Next, a giant thank you to the Ebook Launch team. Dane Low, our book cover designer, created exceptional cover designs for the Right-Minded Teamwork book series. Thank you for elevating Right-Minded Teamwork. (To reach Dane visit EbookLaunch.com.)

Another sincere thank you goes out to Cathi Bosco, our graphic artist, who renovated and modernized many of our Right-Minded Teamwork process models, graphics, and illustrations
(reach her at CathiBosco.com).
And I also want to thank the Media A-Team, who created the original and current versions of the Right Choice Model
(find them at Mediaateam.com).

Finally, I want to express my gratitude to Jackie D'Elia, our website and UX designer, who successfully modernized the RightMindedTeamwork.com website into an easy-to-use platform. Her work allows us to share the RMT books, models, and other resources and materials with the world. Thank you, Jackie.
(Contact Jackie at JackieDElia.com.)

CONTENTS

Foreword 15
   A Message from Reason... 15

Introduction 19
What is Right-Minded Teamwork?... 27
   What Is "Right" in Right-Minded Teamwork? 28
   Overview: Nine Right-Minded Choices 29

Reason, Ego, & the Right-Minded Teamwork Myth 32
   The Myth 33
   Moral of the Story 38

Choice #1 Make the Right-Minded Choice: Choose Reason 55
Choice #2 Oneness or Separateness? Choose to Behave as One............ 61
Choice #3 Right-Minded Communication: Choose to End Separateness 67
Choice #4 Meaningful Vision: Make Your Team's Dream Come True.. 73
Choice #5 Work Agreements: Bring People Together as One 79
Choice #6 Critical Few: Complete Important Tasks First 85
Choice #7 Mistakes Happen: Correct Them; Don't Punish People 91
Choice #8 Conflict Happens: Go to Classroom, Not the Battleground ... 97
Choice #9 Recognition: Make It Easy to Keep Going.......................... 103

Your New Beginning: You Can Work as One 106

Resources 109
  30 Right-Minded Teamwork Attitudes & Behaviors 110
  RMT's 9 Right Choices Survey 123

Glossary of Right-Minded Teamwork Terms & Resources 129
  100% Customer Satisfaction 129
  7 Mindfulness Training Lessons 129
  10 Characteristics of Right-Minded Teammates 130
  12 Steps Workshop Design Process 131
  A Course in Miracles 131
  Accept, Forgive, Adjust 132
  Ally or Adversary Teammate 133
  Avoidance Behavior 134
  Battleground: Where People Are Punished for Mistakes 135
  Certified Master Facilitator (CMF) 136
  Classroom: Where People Learn from Mistakes 136
  Communication Work Agreement 137
  Create, Promote, Allow 138
  Critical Few: Complete Important Tasks First 138
  Decision-Maker: The Real You 139
  Decision-Maker: Trust Your Intuition 140
  Decision-Making Work Agreement 141
  Desire & Willingness: Preconditions for Accountability 142
  Do No Harm. Work as One 143
  Ego & Ego Attack 144
  Interlocking Accountability 145
  Moment of Reason 146
  Onboarding New Teammates 146
  Oneness vs. Separateness 147
  Preventions & Interventions 148

Psychological Goals 149
Reason 150
Reason, Ego & the Right-Minded Teamwork Myth 151
Recognition: Make It Easy to Keep Going................................. 152
Right Choice Model 153
Right-Minded Teamwork's 5-Element Framework 154
Right-Minded Teamwork's 5 Element Implementation Plan....... 155
Right-Minded Teamwork Attitudes & Behaviors 156
Right-Mindedness vs. Wrong-Mindedness 157
RMT Facilitator 158
Team Management System: An RMT Enterprise-Wide Process . 159
Team Operating System & Performance Factor Assessment....... 160
Thought System 161
Train Your Mind.. 162
Uncovering Root Cause.. 163
Unified Circle of Right-Minded Thinking................................. 164
Work Agreements 165

About the Author 167
Books by Dan Hogan.. 170

Praise for Right-Minded Teamwork

A fast read that takes you straight to the root of team dysfunctions and gives you proven, step-by-step tools to improve team function and deliver results. I have paid thousands of dollars for team trainings and workshops that are better summarized here. I am glad to be reminded to choose Reason over Ego and stay in my right mind.

Robin Hensley, VP IT, UPS

The author of this guide is all-knowing and has clearly and in a pithy way documented the nine steps to bringing a team together: that togetherness and one-mindedness are key elements to an average team doing extraordinary things. Your work provides a roadmap to use in building a team that works. Again, thank you. I always enjoyed our time together and appreciated all you did for me and my teams.

Alan Kleier, Former GM/VP, Chevron

In Right-Minded Teamwork, Dan separates the fun and games of team bonding from the hard work (the muck and mire) of team building. He presents an in-depth model for real-world team building in a realistic, direct, and safe manner. This is a book that you will use and wear out. Right-Minded Teamwork is also a support system, providing a rich array of resources.

Patrick Carmichael, VP Best Practices Institute, Former Head Talent Management Saudi Aramco

What's great about the book is that in addition to the process outlined, the author provides supplemental resources and links to additional information to help you out.

Lauren Bailey, Maintenance Superintendent, Chevron

... I successfully used the principles of Right-Minded Teamwork in community mediation. I recommend Right-Minded Teamwork to any mediator engaged in dysfunctional behavior in community mediation.

Rick Murray, JD/Ph.D. Exec. Director Dispute Resolution Center of the Northwest

Foreword

A Message from Reason

Dear Reader,

My name is Reason. We haven't been officially introduced, but I've been your constant supporter for many, many years.

Though you may think of me as an "I," I am not really a separate entity. I live inside of you. I also live inside everyone else, too. For that reason, it is more accurate to say, "We are Reason," collectively.

The Right-Minded Teamwork Myth is a short story that will help you understand what I mean by that.

Here's a little preview:

> *Once, there was only Reason. Everyone had everything they needed, and everyone was happy with what they had.*
>
> *But out of nowhere, a tiny, mad idea crept into our collective minds. For just an instant, we began to wonder,*
>
> *"Is there more to be gained than what we have achieved by working together as one unified team?"*
>
> *This moment was the **birth of separation**.*

> *Fortunately, most of us just kindly laughed off the silly question. But some listened. They began to think separate thoughts. Some had the thought that if they could work alone and take more for themselves, it would make them even happier.*
>
> *Instead of following Reason's advice, they chose to follow Ego (the obvious instigator of such a thought).*
>
> *Because of their choice to break from Reason, teamwork faltered. Choosing to focus only on themselves impacted everyone.*

As you will see in the coming pages, there is more to this story. But even before you read it, allow this excerpt to prepare you. Open your mind to see the true value, importance, and power of *choice* – your choices and the choices of your teammates.

In every situation, every one of us makes a choice to follow either Reason or Ego. The hope, of course, for the sake of your team's success, is that you and your teammates will choose Reason. When you do, you will do no harm, and you will always work as one.

The most beautiful part is that no matter how far you or your teammates may have strayed, by *choosing* to work *with* Reason, you will inevitably find your way back to collaborative, productive teamwork – your pre-separation state.

When following Reason, it is easy for teammates to make Right-Minded choices. It is natural for them to act and behave as a single, unified team, ready to achieve team goals.

This book and the other seven Right-Minded Teamwork books will teach you how to get there. With these tools, you and your team will create and follow your own Right-Minded thought system. You will develop Right-Minded, effective work processes.

Reader, I want you to know that I, Reason, am available to you anytime and anywhere, forever. When you are ready to collaborate and work together as a cohesive team, I will be there, in your mind, prepared to show you the way. Together, we will make it happen. Then, you and your team will easily live the RMT motto. You will **do no harm** and **work as one**.

Join me on the Right-Minded Teamwork journey. A mindful inward journey. One without distance to a goal you want to achieve.

It's your new beginning. Let's start today.

Forever yours,
~ Reason

PS - Don't hesitate to call on me anytime. It only takes a mindful moment. I am always here for you.

Introduction

Hi there! I'm Dan Hogan. I have been in your shoes, wondering how in the world to lead teammates toward greater collaboration and team effectiveness.

In this book, you will find specific actions you can take to achieve better teamwork, or as we call it, Right-Minded Teamwork (RMT). Successful team leaders who consistently create and sustain teams that work as one integrate the essence of the nine, Right-Minded choices into their team, often through team-building workshops.

Because you are reading yet another book on leadership and teamwork, I am confident you have already worked hard to be a good leader. You have probably done so for many reasons. Still, I'm guessing the primary reason is that you've seen, firsthand, how gratifying it is when teammates come together as a collaborative, unified team.

I also assume you know effective teamwork is not just for you and your teammates. It is really for your team's customers.

Despite your efforts, experience, and the knowledge you've gained, I'm sure you've nevertheless experienced your fair share of resistant teammates, dysfunctional bureaucracy, and the like. It can be frustrating when these obstacles diminish your team-building efforts, so much so there were probably times you just wanted to give up and do something else.

But you didn't give up. Something kept pulling you back.

Do you know why you kept at it, refusing to give up? Do you know what that "something" is?

It is your deep-seated desire to help others experience the joy of Right-Minded Teamwork.

You know your teammates and the team's customers will be much better off when teammates understand and apply the principles behind these nine right choices.

Moreover, you know that by extending Right-Minded Teamwork principles to teammates and your customers, you will have made it a win for everyone, including yourself.

You Taught Me These Choices

I started facilitating team-building workshops in 1986. Much has changed since then, but I worked with many talented leaders and teammates, quite like you, even in the early days.

After my first few years, I began to notice these Right-Minded choices emerging in my awareness. I did not invent them. I learned them from people like you.

Observing their effectiveness, I dedicated my career to promoting them and helping teams learn to apply these choices successfully. Today, so many years later, they are still self-evident, self-validating, and universal best practices.

When I published the first edition of this book in 2013, I gave copies to many of my team leader clients. Robin Hensley was one of those talented leaders, and, after reading it, she shared her review:

> *[RMT's 9 Right Choices is] a fast read that takes you straight to the root of team dysfunctions and gives you proven, step-by-step tools to improve team function and deliver results.*
>
> *I have paid thousands of dollars for team trainings and workshops that are better summarized here. I am glad to be reminded to choose Reason over Ego and stay in my right mind.*

Robin Hensley, VP IT, UPS

Robin's was just one of many endorsements I received upon sharing this book. Her response, along with the comments, affirmations, and recommendations from others like her, spoke about the real-world value of these nine concepts and choices.

They affirmed what I had already seen through my years of team building and facilitation efforts: When you persistently include these choices into your team through team-building workshops, your team will improve.

You become a successful Right-Minded Teamwork leader and facilitator. Truly.

With these choices in your mind, you no longer have to wonder what you should do. The answer is always, "**Do no harm**, and **work as one.**"

How to Apply These Choices

There is no one right way to apply these choices, but here is a good plan: Start by reading and understanding all nine choices.

Throughout this book, you will find a *Leader & Teammate Actions* section that outlines specific actions you can take within each choice. By the time you finish reading the last choice, you will know how to apply them.

Here are some possible scenarios:

- You ask all teammates to read this book and complete the survey at the end. Then, you compile teammates' scores and comments and distribute the results to all teammates. As a whole group, you identify the choices you want to apply to your team.
- Alternately, in a team meeting attended by all teammates, you openly discuss the first two of the nine choices. By the end of the session, teammates will have chosen several attitudes and work behaviors to live by going forward.
- For a more thorough application, follow Right-Minded Teamwork's 12-step process to design an RMT-style team-building workshop. (You will learn more about this process at the Glossary of Terms & Resources at the end of this book.)

As you go through the process and begin to apply these choices, trust your intuition. I am confident that you will know the right way to apply them to your team by the time you read and understand them all.

Remember: It Is About the Dialogue

These nine choices are undoubtedly important. But they are secondary to your team's dialogue about them. They will serve as catalysts for your teammate discussions and the eventual creation of team Work Agreements.

Regardless of your approach, every application will include a healthy, functional, and empowering dialogue that moves your teammates toward acting and behaving as one unified team.

. . . . .

Welcome to Your New Role: RMT Leader & Facilitator

Now that you have a clearer sense of the journey we'll be taking together through these pages, I want to take a moment to congratulate you on your new role. Incorporating these 9 Right Choices into your team-building repertoire means you are now a **Right-Minded Teamwork Leader and Facilitator.**

As an RMT Leader and Facilitator, **your specialty is team transformations.**

Using RMT, you help to transform dysfunctional souls into healthy and functional teammates. You guide teammates to convert their mistakes into Right-Minded attitudes and behaviors. They express their deep and heartfelt gratitude for your leadership and facilitation efforts. Some even say you "saved them," continuing to seek your support for years to come.

Whether you're new to team leadership or team facilitation or not, add RMT to your team-building toolkit today. There's no reason not to: All parts of Right-Minded Teamwork, including these 9 Right Choices and Team Work Agreements, are available for your use. There are no licensing or certification requirements.

My only request is that you accept Reason's wisdom on this path. With Reason's guidance, you can easily apply these methods to help your teams create and sustain Right-Minded Teamwork.

My Special Support Function

It took countless workshops, a 35-year career in active team-building facilitation, and the collective wisdom of so many teammates and team leaders to conceptualize and build Right-Minded Teamwork into the robust model it is today.

Though I no longer facilitate actively, choosing to pass that torch on to the next generation of leaders and facilitators, I will always continue to promote Right-Minded Teamwork.

The reason for my continued passion is quite simple. I know, beyond a shadow of a doubt, that Right-Minded Teamwork is right for every team, everywhere, forever. If you use RMT, it *will* help make your teams and the world a better place.

To make that happen, though, **your clients need you to show them and their teams the Right-Minded Teamwork way.**

As you lead them down the RMT path, remember: I am here to support you. So, reach out to me. Ask me questions. Let me get to know you so I can refer you to clients looking for an RMT Leader or Facilitator.

Also remember that even though you will undoubtedly help your teams achieve an "early win," creating and sustaining Right-Minded Teamwork takes at least a year.

So, as you enter into the team-building process, stick with it for the long haul. Plan to stay with your team(s) for at least one to two years. Help them firmly establish RMT in their team. Give them the foundation they need to learn, grow, and succeed.

As you do, you will do your part to make the world a better place for everyone, everywhere, forever.

Let's get started now.

Dan Hogan

What is Right-Minded Teamwork?

> *Right-Minded Teamwork is a business-oriented, psychological approach to team building where **acceptance, forgiveness**, and **adjustment** are teammate characteristics, and 100% customer satisfaction is the team's result.*

Right-Minded Teamwork is practical. It produces positive business results by getting real work done. Above all, it naturally motivates teammates to grow.

At the core of RMT is a simple concept applicable to teams of all sizes: **Do No Harm. Work as One.**

A Right-Minded Teammate can be firm, direct, gentle, and compassionate at the same time. They don't blame themselves or others. They are allies, not adversaries.

Instead, they **accept, forgive,** and **adjust** their attitudes and behaviors. They seek solutions to team mistakes and look for ways to improve difficult situations.

Right-Minded Teammates do no harm, they work as one, and they sincerely believe that "none of us is as smart as all of us."

What Is "Right" in Right-Minded Teamwork?

RMT has nothing to do with right-brain thinking or right-wing viewpoints.

It has everything to do with what your team, together, decides is "right." Your team's choices, identified collectively, define your team's Right-Minded Teamwork.

> *The "right" way is the way you choose is right for your team.*

So, how do you open up a team discussion about what is right or wrong for your team?

- You learn about Right-Minded Teamwork by discussing these nine choices.
- You apply some or all of the tools and exercises offered here.
- You can also use the list of Right-Minded Attitudes & Behaviors listed in the Resources section of this book as a guide for embracing ally versus adversarial characteristics.

To achieve Right-Minded Teamwork, your team must begin by agreeing on which choice to apply first. Then, gradually, you can apply more choices over time.

Overview:
Nine Right-Minded Choices

These are the nine essential Right-Minded choices:

1. Once your team has committed to achieving Right-Minded Teamwork, **there is no difficulty in making a Right-Minded choice.**

2. **Choosing RMT and choosing to behave as one unified team are foundational choices** for all the other nine choices.

   Your team will not live these first two choices perfectly right away. Nevertheless, making a wholehearted commitment is a necessary first step.

   Be patient but persistent. Move toward your team's definition of Right-Minded Teamwork by conducting continuous improvement workshops every three months.

3. **Right-Minded communication, which is effective and kind, flows effortlessly** from those who are committed to and who actively live the first two choices.

4. **A meaningful team vision provides the context** for choosing Right-Minded behaviors plus your team's continuous improvement operating system.

5. A team that **actively lives its Work Agreements** is a team that has established an environment in which teammates forgive past mistakes in the present, which increases the likelihood of the team achieving its full potential in the future.

6. Right-Minded teams **complete their critical few tasks first**.

7. **Correcting mistakes is natural and safe for Right-Minded teammates** because they know that doing so is one of the most sensible ways to learn.

8. When **team conflict** occurs, and it will, **Right-Minded teammates** psychologically rise above the Ego's battleground and then offer constructive solutions.

9. **Giving and receiving authentic recognition** for a job well-done feeds team spirit and fuels the Right-Minded Teamwork process.

. . . . .

Below is a more detailed explanation of these nine choices.

Before we go deeper, I want to introduce you to three personalities: **Reason**, **Ego**, and the **Decision-Maker**. Each of these three entities plays a vital role in your journey to building a team that works as one.

EGO

DECISION MAKER

REASON

Reason, Ego, & the Right-Minded Teamwork Myth

The Right-Minded Teamwork Myth is a story that illustrates how teamwork originally functioned and how it got to where it is today.

Achieving the story's mythological ideals is not entirely possible. However, adopting these ideal attitudes and behaviors as team goals is not only possible, it's practical.

Adopting these behaviors is your team's first step in choosing a set of Right-Minded attitudes. (For examples, see the list of Right-Minded Teamwork Attitudes & Behaviors in the Resources section.)

The second step is to discuss and define the behaviors that demonstrate your chosen attitudes. Those choices are described behaviorally in your team Work Agreements.

The third and final step is to live and follow your Work Agreements, day in and day out.

Applying Right-Minded attitudes and behaviors will move you closer to Right-Minded Teamwork, which will result in satisfied customers. Right-Minded Teamwork is a win for everyone.

The Myth

Once, before we lived in tribes, we all naturally worked together as one.

All our needs were met. There was no sense of want because there was no need. Peace, abundance, and collaboration were normal. Instead of "yours" and "mine," we shared with each other simply and effortlessly.

There was no leader, either, but there was a clear, guiding spirit that emanated from our collective cooperation. We named that shepherding spirit **Reason**. Reason continually and gently reminded us of our caring thoughts and feelings for one another.

With Reason's guidance, there was no fear. There was no doubt as to who and what we were. We were one, always there for one another. We easily worked together. We needed and wanted each other. We had everything we could ask for.

But out of nowhere, a tiny, mad idea crept into our collective minds. For just an instant, we began to wonder,

> *Is there more to be gained than what we have achieved by working together as one unified team?*

This moment was the **birth of separation**.

Fortunately, most of us just kindly laughed off the silly question. But some listened. They began to think separate thoughts. Some had the thought that if they could work alone and take more for themselves, it would make them even happier.

Then Reason stepped gently into our collective minds and asked,

> *But how could we have more than everything?*

Reason went on to remind us that we had free will. If we wanted, we could follow that foolish little thought. If we did, it would be just like falling asleep and having a bad dream. Fortunately, Reason assured us that if anyone fell asleep, we would not abandon them. All of us would remain here together, as one, to help them wake up.

For most of us, Reason's gentle question and kind words made sense. We decided Reason's advice was right for us. That decision was our first **moment of Reason**. Shifting our focus back to our teamwork, we continued to work together as one.

But not everyone agreed.

One, named **"Ego,"** concluded that if they had more than anyone else, it would make them even more special than Reason - or so they thought.

Ego didn't realize that this idea of being different and special was yet *another tiny, mad idea*. In the world of Oneness, everyone is on the same team, working towards the same goals for the same reasons, contributing fully. There is no value in being an outlier, somehow different than the rest. What would that add to the team? Within the Unified Circle of Right-Minded Thinking, we are all one.

Still, Ego persisted, following the mad idea, and seeking their own way until they began to fall asleep, just as Reason had predicted. As Ego's eyes closed, Reason tenderly placed a folded note alongside Ego. On the outside, it read, "Open when you are ready to wake up." On the inside, Reason included practical ideas on how to move back into the Unified Circle of Right-Minded Thinking. Eventually, this vital information would help Ego return.

But let's continue with the story. Fast asleep, Ego didn't notice Reason's gesture or note. To the slumbering Ego, the plan was crystal clear: Get more by taking more from others—more of... everything.

So off Ego went, taking more and more. Even though there was enough for everyone, Ego continued to take extra. But soon, Ego ran into a problem: Where to store all the extra stuff so no one would take it back?

Ego decided to leave and find a place to hide the stuff, somewhere no one could see it or steal it.

Proud of having such an excellent plan, Ego struck up a conversation with some others on the way to taking more stuff to hide. Ego bragged about all the really good stuff already stored away and the excellent plan to acquire even more. Ego even claimed to have more than Reason, which of course, was not true. Ego's illusion - *delusion* - made Ego feel special and important.

Regrettably, Ego was able to convince a few others to join in. They wanted Ego's version of specialness, too. Each of them began taking more, just like Ego.

They called their new group a tribe. Reason, and all those still following Reason's attitudes and Right-Minded Thinking, called them the Separated Ones. For a little while, the separated tribe sort of worked... until one day, a tribe member took stuff from another tribe member.

Now there was conflict. Conflict was a new feeling; no one had experienced it before. Other new emotions, like anger, fear, revenge, grievance, and doubt, began showing up in the tribe members' minds as well. Everyone agreed these new feelings were awful. They convinced themselves and each other that their only hope of getting rid of those dreadful feelings was to go out and take more stuff. They tried to cover their fear with *more* - which, in truth, never works.

Soon, the tribe member who lost stuff to the other member became incredibly angry and hostile. They couldn't stand it any longer. A new question crept in: How could they each protect their stuff?

One more tiny, mad, Ego-driven idea arose in their mind:

> *I know what I'll do! I'll leave this tribe and start my own tribe.*

From that moment on, more and more tribe members began to join and split off, then join and split again, over and over. Eventually, their wrong-minded choices created the world we live in today: a world filled with adversaries where once there were only allies.

Today, we have thousands of tribes around the globe taking from one another in more physical and psychological ways than we can possibly count. We live in a complex world of duality and chaos. A world of yours and mine. A world where, far too often, people fight over and take each other's stuff.

Most of us who are stuck in wrong-minded thought systems do not even know we are stuck. Fortunately, as napping Egos, we are only asleep in a nightmarish and chaotic dream where every choice leads to greater dysfunction.

We are dreaming of separation, but in reality, we are still one. If we choose, we can still follow Reason. We can begin our journey back to Right-Minded Teamwork and the unified circle of Oneness. It's not too late to wake up.

Waking up means first gently accepting the fact that, as long as we view ourselves as our Egos, we are *out of our right minds*.

Once we accept this - our first **moment of Reason** as a separated tribe member - we will discover Reason's note, apply the sage advice, and gladly embrace Right-Minded attitudes and behaviors.

Moral of the Story

Wake up.

Shift your perspective.

Return to the Unified Circle of Right-Minded Thinking.

No matter what happens, and no matter how real it may feel or appear, Ego's world is a dream. As a team leader, teammate, or team facilitator, **your new purpose** is to partner with Reason to awaken your teammates from their negative, adversarial nightmare and show them how to choose Reason, too.

As you do, you will invite them to participate in creating your team's Right-Minded thought system. This set of team beliefs and behaviors will bring all teammates back into collaborative unity, allowing you to work together as one team.

Reason, Ego & You – the Decision-Maker

Three entities within you influence your daily choices as a Right-Minded Teammate. These three are **Ego, Reason**, and the **Decision-Maker.**

Ego and Reason are your teachers and guides. The Decision Maker is the part of you that decides who you will listen to and follow.

You, the Decision-Maker, are a student in life's classroom. This classroom takes many forms. Your team is one of them.

As the Decision-Maker, **you always have free will** to follow either Reason or Ego. It is your choice, and only yours.

Because you have free will, you are 100% responsible for what you think and choose to do. Each morning, whether you are conscious of it or not, your Decision-Maker decides what kind of day you will have by choosing which teacher to follow: Ego or Reason.

Ego is a negative influence who believes your team is like a battleground. Ego is continuously talking inside your mind, urgently telling you it's a desperate and dangerous world out there. You hear that people are murderous and out to get you. Ego reminds you that it is everyone else's fault (not yours!) that you are stuck in this constant battle, endlessly suffering within your team.

Ego is a noisy, wrong-minded teacher, telling you to attack and blame. And if you don't listen and follow Ego's thought system and do what you've been told, Ego attacks and blames you for not adhering to their advice.

At work, your Ego sees all your team's challenges and encourages you to respond with attack or blame. Ego sounds like,

> *I can't believe they've all screwed this up. How could you be such an idiot as to stand with them? I said they were out to get you. We should have done our own thing. I told you they were going to blame you for this.*

Reason, on the other hand, follows a different thought system. Reason is quiet, gentle, and kind. Reason is ready to partner with you to show you how to behave in a Right-Minded, collaborative way.

Reason knows you and your teammates will be much better off when you rise above the battleground and work together as a unified team. According to Reason, your team is a wonderful and safe classroom where you re-learn how to live and work as one.

REASON

Reason waits quietly while Ego rants, causing fear, guilt, and anxiety to mount inside you.

If it gets too painful, you, the Decision-Maker, say to yourself,

There must be a better way! We need better teamwork!

Expressing your genuine desire for change means you are ready for a **moment of Reason**. As you open your mind, looking for a new way, Reason steps in gently. You begin to wake up. You remember the attitudes and behaviors you long ago committed to living before you followed Ego's advice and fell into the dream.

As those Right-Minded attitudes and behaviors return to you, you soon find better ways to work and interact with your teammates. Together, you grow and evolve, making your collective experience and results better for everyone.

Trust Your Intuition as the Decision-Maker

If thinking about Reason and Ego is new to you, it can be helpful to think of Reason as your positive intuition and Ego as your negative, arrogant, and sometimes vindictive intuition.

At different times throughout our lives, we all listen to and follow each of these teachers.

Stop and remember when you had a hunch or a feeling as to what you should do or say in a particular situation. Did you ignore your intuition? Let's say you did not follow your instinct, and it turned out to be a mistake. What did you say to yourself and others?

> *I wish I had trusted my intuition!*

As this memory illustrates, **you already know how to listen and be mindful** of your intuition. It is your natural, pre-separation state of mind. You just need to do it regularly.

If not…

Remember a time when you became angry, agitated, or annoyed with a teammate. Without thinking, you said mean-spirited things. You, too, were saying to yourself, *"My life can't get better until you change."*

Accept it. Your negative behavior happened because you did not stop for a **moment of Reason**.

*You were literally **out of your right mind** as you unconsciously turned towards Ego for guidance.*

During your reaction, you were mindless as you followed Ego's advice. Then, after a while, once you stepped back and calmed down, you could see your behavior was a mistake - *only* a mistake, to be corrected, not punished. At this moment, you shifted your perspective. You forgave yourself, and you adjusted by apologizing and promising not to behave that way again. You returned to your right mind.

If you are not accustomed to trusting your intuition but would like to do so more, you will need to practice.

*The key is to **pause**, be **still**, and intentionally **listen** for your positive intuition - that **moment of Reason** - before you react to a situation or event.*

It is that simple. But that does not make it easy, especially at first. It takes mindful practice to train your mind to listen for this joyous, intuitive moment. It takes an unwavering commitment to stop yourself continually, gently, and compassionately when you become angry, fearful, agitated, or anxious.

It is not always easy, but it can be done. Many have learned this skill. You can, too. As the Decision-Maker, you always have free will regarding whether you choose to follow Ego or Reason. Even if you've tried before and failed, you can start again today.

Remember that even with steadfast commitment, it will take practice to excel. You will make mistakes. That's okay. Choose Reason again. Choose to follow your Work Agreements again. And again. When you realize you've chosen Ego, apologize, forgive, correct, forget the mistake and move on. The more you practice, the easier it will get.

You will soon find that as you change your mind, you automatically change your behavior. And when you change your behavior, you transform your team into a lovely learning classroom. The more you make an effort to *be* **in your right mind**, the easier it will become to *stay* **in your right mind**.

Now, instead of saying, *"I wish I had listened to my intuition,"* you will say,

> *I'm so glad I turned to Reason and followed my intuition!*

DECISION MAKER

REASON

You Have Only Two Response Choices

The **Right-Minded Choice Model** teaches that you are the **Decision-Maker**, and you only have two choices regarding how you respond to every difficult situation.

When a challenging situation happens, you either:
- accept Ego's guidance and act like a victim or victimizer, or
- embrace Reason and act in an accountable, Right-Minded way which is described in your team Work Agreements.

Even though there are many variations of those two choices, *there are still just two.*

At all times, you are mindful, or you are mindless. You are either following your Right Mind, **Reason**, or your wrong mind, **Ego**.

   *To Learn More...*

To learn more, go to RightMindedTeamwork.com or your favorite book retailer and pick up your copy of *How to Apply the Right Choice Model: Create a Right-Minded Team That Works as One.*

Mindfulness *Is* Choice in Action

When you are mindless, you don't think or reflect. Instead of consciously choosing how to respond, you react unconsciously in an emotionally immature way, blaming others or avoiding the situation altogether.

When you're mindful, you reflect and carefully choose how you respond to everything that happens to you and around you. When a problematic situation happens, being mindful means asking yourself this question that is in the model:

What did I do or say to **create, promote,** *or* **allow** *this to happen?*

Your answers to this question help you and your team experience a **moment of Reason**, which paves the way for you to create successful solutions.

As an example, let's assume a significant mistake has happened in your team.

Half the team is aggressively blaming the other half for the mistake in what is often called an **"Ego attack."**

> RIGHT-MINDED
> **Accountability**
> is the **desire, willingness,** and **ability** to change my mind & behavior in order to effectively respond to difficult situations.
>
> This means owning my part in the situation by asking:
>
> *"How did I CREATE, PROMOTE, or ALLOW this difficult situation to happen?"*
>
> RightMindedTeamwork.com

Teammates are making toxic and hurtful statements, directly and indirectly, about each other. The team is stuck in a battleground of "attack and defend." No one is working to resolve the mistake.

Seeking a **moment of Reason**, you ask yourself,

> *What am I doing to create, promote, or allow this blaming conversation to continue?*

You realize you've been standing by and saying nothing. You were **avoiding**, which is the **first step in the lower loop** of the Right Choice Model.

Now that you are aware of your attitude and behavior, you change your mind. You choose to follow Reason and act in a Right-Minded, accountable way, just as your **Work Agreement** states.

Reason is that part of your mind that always speaks for Right Choice attitudes and behaviors. When you are looking for a **moment of Reason** and want to find the best way to respond to a difficult team situation, say to yourself:

> *I am here to be truly helpful.*
>
> *I am here to represent Reason who sent me.*
>
> *I do not have to worry about what to say or what to do because Reason, who sent me, will direct me.*

Then remember your two Right-Minded options, which are likely part of your Work Agreements:
- Engage in helpful, problem-solving communication.
- Advocate that teammates correct mistakes rather than punish and blame.

Holding these two options in your mind and heart, you wait for Reason's direction. With your focus on Reason, **intuitive** answers easily come. Once you have received Reason's advice, in a calm, "do-no-harm-work-as-one" voice, you say,

> *Here's a suggestion. Let's discuss what we know, the facts, about what happened. Then let's find an immediate solution.*
>
> *After we resolve the mistake, let's have a second team discussion, not to blame, but to create a Work Agreement so that this mistake doesn't happen again. How does that sound?*

If you had followed Ego's advice instead of Reason's and continued your **avoidance behavior**, the conflict would have continued.

Since you chose to look towards Reason, you created an environment where you and your teammates **recovered** from the mistake, the **final step in the upper loop** of the Choice Model.

Reason, as always, has brought you - and hopefully everyone else, too - **back into your Right Mind.**

By listening to Reason, trusting your intuition, and following your **Work Agreements**, you effectively train your mind to consistently return to the Unified Circle of Right-Minded Thinking.

Return to the Unified Circle of Right-Minded Thinking

When your team discusses and agrees on your psychological goals – your consciously chosen set of attitudes and behaviors as described in your Work Agreements – you have created your team's collective thought system.

By uniting with each other in this way and openly committing to one another through your Work Agreements, you are renouncing Ego in yourself and your teammates and collectively committing to train your minds to follow Reason.

This process of creating team Work Agreements is your undivided declaration of interdependence. Together, you are saying,

> *We hold these mindful truths to be self-evident, that all minds are created equal, and whosoever believes it will have everlasting freedom to choose Right-Minded teamwork.*

Your declaration, combined with your daily acts of living your team Work Agreements, *is your return* to the forgiving Unified Circle of Right-Minded Thinking. It is taking ownership of the one fundamental freedom that no one can take away from you: your **freedom to choose** how to respond to life's challenges.

At every moment, your Decision-Maker is making that choice in one of two ways: Either your Decision-Maker is choosing based on Reason's Right-Minded principles and your team's **Work Agreements** or Ego's wrong-minded dictates.

> *Follow Reason, and you declare your freedom from Ego's battlefields.*
>
> *Follow Reason, and you have joined others who hold these Right-Minded thoughts to be self-evident and true.*
>
> *Follow Reason, and you transform your fixed perspectives by reinterpreting attack behaviors as a call for help – your help.*
>
> *Follow Reason, and your team will agree on a Right-Minded set of attitudes and behaviors as described in your **Work Agreements**.*
>
> *By following **Reason** and your **Work Agreements**, you will renounce Ego while uniting with your fellow teammates.*
>
> *Do this, and you will return to your ultimate goal, the forgiving Unified Circle of Right-Minded Thinking.*

Reason's Personal Note to You

Do you remember in the Right-Minded Teamwork Myth when, as Ego was falling asleep, Reason tenderly placed a folded note alongside Ego? On the outside, it read, *"Open when you are ready to wake up."* On the inside were practical ideas on how to move back into the Unified Circle of Right-Minded Thinking.

Now that you are ready to wake up and help your teammates wake up, too, it is time to read what Reason wrote. You unfold the note and read...

. . . . .

We are Reason

Before you listened to Ego and embraced the tiny, mad idea of separation, everyone stood inside the Unified Circle of Right-Minded Thinking. We were One. We were, collectively, Reason.

You know this to be true. Your own experience has taught you this. There have been times, even in your separated life, when all your needs were met. There was no sense of want because you had what you needed. That experience reflects your pre-separation state.

You have also felt, in the past, safe and secure in Reason's way of living and working with your brothers and sisters.

Remember those moments of Reason. Restore your mind to Reason, follow your intuition, shift your perspective, and your Right-Minded behaviors will tenderly flow through you to your teammates.

Of course, to simply say these words means nothing. You must live these words. Then, they will mean everything.

Choose to step inside the Right-Minded circle of unified teamwork and gently and firmly train your mind and heart to remember your pre-separation state. Say to yourself, "I can elect to change all thoughts of separation. Choosing anything but working together as one unified team is nothing but a dream."

This is the truth.

Within your team and within yourself, it must be said, then repeated many times. At first, it will be accepted as partially true with many reservations. Over time, it will be considered seriously, more and more, until it is finally accepted as truth.

Come back!

Stand confidently inside the circle. Draw your teammates back into living Right-Minded Teamwork behaviors. By drawing your teammates back, you strengthen Reason's way of living in this world for your brother, your sister, and yourself.

Now, follow these instructions. Apply the 5 Elements of Right-Minded Teamwork and the 9 Right Choices. Learn the 7 Mindfulness Lessons of Right-Minded Thinking. And begin your journey back to the place of Oneness from which you came.

~ Reason

This story, the Right-Minded Teamwork process, the Right-Minded Teamwork Attitudes & Behaviors, and the RMT Choice Model were inspired by *A Course in Miracles*.

*Right-Minded Teamwork is a learning process
performed daily in your work-life classroom.*

Your teammates are your classmates.

Your teachers are Reason and Ego.

*The Decision-Maker, the part of you that chooses,
always chooses to follow either Ego or Reason.*

*You are free to believe what you choose.
What you choose to do
reflects what you think and believe.*

*Reason teaches you to think this way:
Do No Harm. Work as One.*

Choose to follow Reason.

*This is the first Right Choice.
The eight other choices all rest on this one.*

Choice #1
Make the Right-Minded Choice: Choose Reason

Choosing Reason: A Foundational Choice

Once you and your teammates agree to continue the daily practice of following Reason's Right-Minded Teamwork choices, you cannot fail to create a team that works as one.

This choice is necessary because it is the foundation upon which all the other choices stand.

The one fundamental freedom that no one can take away from you is your freedom to choose how to respond to life's challenges. At every moment, your Decision-Maker is making that choice, in one of two ways. Either your Decision-Maker is choosing based on Reason's Right-Minded principles or Ego's wrong-minded rules.

It may be hard to accept that you have only two options, Reason or Ego, but it is true. However, realizing there are hundreds of variations of those two choices can make it easier.

Still, all the choices you make stem from one fundamental truth: Your behavior comes from what your Decision-Maker chooses to think. Depending on whether you choose to follow Reason or Ego, you will find yourself in either a place of Right-Mindedness or wrong-mindedness.

Claim Your Freedom

To claim your freedom, you must train your mind to listen and follow Reason's teachings, especially when difficult situations happen. By doing so, you will be thinking in an emotionally mature, responsible, and accountable way.

If I told you to think and behave the same unproductive way, repeatedly, and that I wanted you to produce different, high-quality results each time, you would either tell me I was foolish or asking the impossible. You would not just blindly do the unproductive thing, over and over. You would not knowingly make no progress, and then, when it came time to show your results, try to excuse your inability to deliver by saying you could not help it.

*But this is exactly what you are doing **if you repeatedly excuse yourself for wrong-minded thinking.***

How will you know if you are excusing wrong-minded thinking? Your relationships will reflect it. Our relationships are an *outward picture of our inward condition.*

If your relationships are in turmoil, it is a sure sign you are living your life more often from your wrong mind.

If your relationships are enriching and heartening, then you are likely following Reason's guidance.

To bring more Right-Minded experiences into your life, consider your workplace as your classroom.

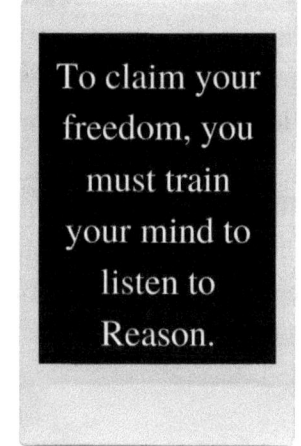

To claim your freedom, you must train your mind to listen to Reason.

Embrace your teammates as your fellow students. Acknowledge that Reason and Ego are your two teachers. Go to class every day with hope and faith in your mind, knowing that when you let go of any form of Ego attack, you will learn joyful lessons from Reason.

As soon as you are ready to be part of a team that acts as one, you will find Reason ready to help you. Until then, Reason will wait patiently for you to awaken whenever you change your mind.

As you learn, remember that no one follows one teacher all the time. Most of us are continually moving back and forth between Ego and Reason. If you find it's true for you, too, don't worry. It does not make you a bad person. You are merely confused and conflicted because you sometimes listen to and follow your Ego.

When this happens, and you are having an unconscious, habitual Ego attack, your task is to gently remind yourself that you are simply and temporarily out of your Right Mind.

As soon as you become conscious and aware of your options, you can shift into a moment of Reason.

In this instant of Reason, you stop and still yourself. You remember your previously chosen Right-Minded attitudes, the ones you chose in advance in your team Work Agreements to guide you when an Ego attack happens. Looking within, you renounce Ego and ask Reason for guidance as to how to respond to the difficult situation. Because you are genuinely listening, you hear Right-Minded, reasonable solutions.

Now, operating from Reason, you demonstrate Right-Minded behaviors. You unify with your teammates through your Work Agreements, and you help yourself and your teammates create and sustain a team that works as one.

Your joining is your *declaration of interdependence.*

It is your return to your team's Unified Circle of Right-Minded Thinking.

It is your affirmation that all minds are created equal and your belief that you all have the everlasting freedom to choose Right-Minded Teamwork.

Choose Right-Minded Teamwork, and you will always **do no harm** and **work as one**. It is that simple. Though it is not always easy, it is always that simple.

Leader & Teammate Actions

In a team meeting, all teammates discuss the cost and benefit of making the Right Choice: choosing Reason over Ego. This is an aspirational dialogue that is typically a short discussion. It usually ends with all teammates saying, *"Of course, we want to behave maturely and responsibly."*

Though this desirable conclusion may be obvious, you must have this discussion that leads to everyone's public commitment to choose Reason over Ego.

Once you do, the natural next step will be to discuss the second of the 9 Right Choices, which we will review next. In this second discussion, the team will define what behaving in a "mature and responsible way" means to them. In that dialogue, teammates will agree on their unique set of Right-Minded attitudes and behaviors, which will soon become known as your team's chosen thought system.

Living these chosen attitudes and behaviors is how each teammate publicly demonstrates their commitment to choosing Reason over Ego.

*You and your teammates have a pivotal choice:
Believe and behave as one team,
or pull in separate directions.*

*Separateness hinders performance.
It encourages little to no collaboration, reinforces
power struggles, feeds the feeling of helplessness, and
justifies finger-pointing and blame.*

*Oneness helps performance.
It creates collaboration, empowers people
to take accountability, and perhaps,
most importantly, creates trust and safety,
which is the condition for Choice #3.*

The cost and benefits are clear.

*Only Oneness will allow you to
do no harm and work as one.*

Choose Oneness.

Choice #2
Oneness or Separateness?
Choose to Behave as One

Choosing to Behave as One

Choose Oneness.

If you don't, teammates who have self-serving, arrogant, or even selfish Egos will overrun you to create more teammate separateness.

Successful teams behave as one. Their members immerse themselves in team goals and think of themselves as allies and extensions of each other, not as adversaries with separate, selfish interests.

Teammates on teams that work as one continuously correct attitudes and behaviors in themselves that do not support Oneness. They create and follow a collaborative team operating system. They believe they are allies. They sincerely desire for every team member to succeed.

You are instinctively drawn to teams that work as one.

Stop for a moment and consider this truth. You will know it is true because your own experience has taught you. Think of any successful group you have witnessed, such as a theatrical

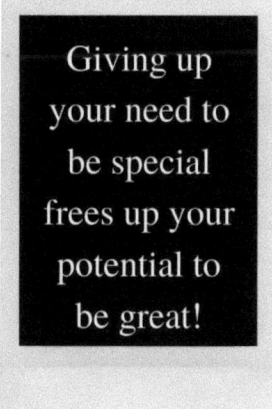

Giving up your need to be special frees up your potential to be great!

troupe or an Olympic sports team. The contributions of individuals combine seamlessly into a flawless, almost magical performance. Watching such acts, and better yet participating in them, inspires you and touches your heart.

You like hearing about, talking about, and interacting with teams like these. You naturally want more. In fact, you are innately attracted to being in a state of Oneness with your teammates.

So, what prevents teams from achieving Oneness?

A simple answer is fear, the fear of losing perceived specialness.

That fear stems from what appears to be a war inside you.

On one side is your **Ego**, the inner voice that vigorously promotes separateness and specialness. Your Ego strongly and loudly says, *"If you commit to this team, it will swallow you up, and you'll be lost. You won't matter anymore, only the team. Your financial needs will not be met. You will not be special. You must fight for what is rightfully yours, or it will not be worth it to you."* Teammates become adversaries because of this wrong-minded thinking.

On the other side is **Reason**, the advocate for **Oneness**.

Reason is patient and kind, gently making a case for choosing Oneness. Though the Ego wants the inner struggle to feel like war, Reason never steps into the battleground with the Ego. Instead, Reason waits, and when you are ready to listen, Reason offers a different perspective: *"Giving up your need to be special frees up your potential to be great."*

Reason's clarity and continuous, gentle call for unity are calming. Reason's thought system makes sense. No one can do everything; pulling apart and working towards separate, selfish interests cannot achieve the goal.

Listen to this closely: There is no war inside you unless you follow Ego. Teammates become allies by embracing Reason's Right-Minded Thinking.

So, take a stand. Choose to side with Reason. Become part of a team that works as one and leave behind the divisive belief that separate goals and selfish interests are somehow beneficial.

Leader & Teammate Actions

For teammates, living Right-Minded attitudes and behaviors every day is a demonstration of choosing Oneness over separateness, choosing Reason over Ego, and doing no harm while working as one.

For this to be possible, all teammates must first agree on your team's set of Right-Minded Attitudes & Behaviors in a team meeting.

Before the meeting, it is wise to ask teammates to review the list of Right-Minded Attitudes & Behaviors listed in the Resources section of this book. Ask everyone to choose their favorite and come to the meeting prepared to discuss and answer these questions:

1. Why will our team benefit from living and following these choices?
2. I believe that living these choices will ensure we create a team that works as one unified team for these reasons: _____.

During the meeting, everyone shares their favorite choice. The team chooses at least three attitudes and behaviors to guide them going forward.

*Right-Minded communication
is Reason's primary method
for ending separateness.*

Right-Minded Teamwork communication:

- *Affirms Oneness*
- *Publicizes your vision*
- *Simplifies Work Agreements*
- *Clarifies team tasks*
- *Facilitates corrections*
- *Strengthens team relationships*
- *Points to the classroom*
- *Conveys genuine recognition*

Right-Minded communication is vital for ensuring teammates are working toward achieving bottom-line business results.

Right-Minded communication is essential for building and sustaining a team that does no harm and works as one.

Choice #3
Right-Minded Communication: Choose to End Separateness

Right-Minded Communication

"Mindedness" describes what you think.

What you think moves you in one of two ways. Either you move toward Reason's way of working as a unified team, or you move in the direction of Ego and separateness, created by team conflict.

But what you think is not all you are. What you think was formed in your childhood and strengthened in your adulthood. Your thoughts are the combination of your education, your culture, and your primal instinct to survive physically and psychologically.

Your thoughts are also the cause of your communication style. Therefore, the way you communicate is the result of what you choose to think.

Teams that work as one seek out opportunities to improve communication. When they find them, they take action.

> Everything you do involves some form of communication. Reason's communication style is best.

For example, successful teammates know their vision will not continue to inspire them if it is not discussed and kept in their line of sight. They know their job performance will suffer if they do not continually dialogue about new and better ways to perform their work. They also know their team spirit will suffer if they do not stop long enough to celebrate and publicize successes.

They recognize the value of Right-Minded communication, so they work on it every chance they get.

Right-Minded Communication: Your Responsibility

To create Right-Minded communication, you can do three things right now.

1. Look honestly within yourself. Spot the Ego-directed thoughts and choices you are currently experiencing. Use the Right-Minded Teamwork Attitudes & Behaviors list in the Resources section if you need to. And then let them go.

   Remember, what you say to yourself and others is a reflection of what you think. If you are holding grievances, injustices, or fear in your mind, your communication will reflect it. And, when your language reflects wrong-minded thinking, you will create conflict, whether you are aware of it or not.

2. Ask the people you respect to give you feedback on your communication style.

   Communication comes in many forms – tone, body language, word choice, listening, speaking, and even silence play a role. Ask others to describe your style, then decide what you want to improve.

3. Ask your team to create and follow a communication Work Agreement.

   A common type of example would be one that describes how the team will communicate when individuals disagree.

Remember, it is impossible to communicate alone; everything you do in your team involves some form of communication. For that reason, it is wise to focus on improving how you and your teammates communicate.

Better communication means you can easily **do no harm** while you **work as one**.

Leader & Teammate Actions

In a team meeting, all teammates will agree on a communication team Work Agreement.

Before the meeting, it is wise to ask teammates to answer the following questions. Instruct them to bring their ideas to the team meeting where you will together create a communication Work Agreement.

1. Why should our team improve communication?
2. What communications are working well? What communications need improvement?
3. Why should I improve my communication? What are the costs? What are the costs if I do nothing?

If your team does not have experience creating Work Agreements (for more on Work Agreements, see Choice #5), then the leader will share the following Starter Communication Work Agreement. Afterward, the teammates share and discuss their answers to the questions above. Next, the team might edit this starter Agreement so it specifically fits them and describes their preferred communication style.

Communication Work Agreement: Starter Version

Team Choice - Intention:
1. Each team member will communicate their thoughts and feelings in an appropriate way.

Clarifications / Conditions for Acceptance:
   A. We follow the spirit and intent of our company values and team psychological goals.
   B. "Appropriate" can reference tone of voice, word choice, body language, being assertive versus aggressive, etc. Here are examples to live by: _____, _____, _____ (write them down).
   C. If we feel or believe another person is being inappropriate, we will _____ (describe how you will confront them).
   D. Even though this Agreement describes inappropriate behaviors, we also agree to give positive reinforcement. To do that, we will _____.
   E. Not only do we agree to hold ourselves accountable, but we will hold others accountable in a safe and supportive way, such as _____ (describe the behaviors of holding someone accountable).
   F. (Insert other conditions or clarifications)
   G. If a team member continues to break this Agreement, we will _____ (describe the steps of how you will confront that person).

For more about team Work Agreements, go to your favorite book retailer or RigthMindedTeamwork.com, and search for ***How to Facilitate Team Work Agreements****: A Practical, 10-Step Process for Building a Right-Minded Team That Works as One.*

Extraordinary teams believe in more than just strategic plans and financial goals.

They feel an instinctive passion for accomplishing their team's vision.

But people will not and cannot fully invest themselves in their work unless they genuinely believe it is worthwhile and makes a positive difference for others and themselves.

To Do No Harm and Work as One, they need a meaningful vision.

Remember, Martin Luther King, Jr. said,

"I have a dream."

He did not say he had a strategic plan.

Choice #4
Meaningful Vision: Make Your Team's Dream Come True

Creating Passion Through Meaningful Vision

If teammates say, *"Sure, we have a vision, but I can't remember exactly what it is,"* you can be assured there is little passion for achieving that vision.

Authentic team passion creates a powerful driving force that establishes team focus and makes things happen. A meaningful vision gives team members a mountaintop view of where the team is going and where it has been.

Vision channels the team's energy toward accomplishing the critical few tasks. This focus decreases the likelihood of the team getting diverted or distracted by the trivial many tasks. For this reason, team visions are crucial. But a vision without passion is a statement soon forgotten.

The way in which your team goes about creating its vision is just as important as the vision itself.

A vision without passion is a statement that is soon forgotten.

Why? Because creating a team vision is a soul-searching exercise of sorting out all the options, uncovering just the right elements to create the necessary spark, providing clarity, and achieving true buy-in from team members.

It is the genuine alignment of intentions and hopes that naturally inspires teams to greatness. A sterile, hastily-crafted vision statement cannot do this.

Some team leaders, after listening to their Ego, avoid involving the team in creating a vision. They fear that if they allow people to explore what could be, teammates will not want to do what the leader wants them to do.

Reason says the opposite.

Reason says that when you assimilate individual teammate hopes into the team's vision, it inspires collaboration and passion. With collaboration and passion, the team leverages an overwhelming reservoir of creative, do-no-harm, get-it-done behavior.

Reason also tells you that Right-Minded Teamwork does not just happen without persistent effort. Therefore, every team needs to establish a continuous-improvement operating system that includes periodic team-building workshops.

When teammates have a meaningful vision plus an effective continuous improvement operating system, they create a team that not only sees as one but works as one.

Is your team passionate about its vision? Are your teammates excited about the journey ahead? Does your team have a continuous-improvement operating system?

If the answers to these questions are anything but yes, stop right now. Focus your efforts on creating a vision that naturally inspires every person on your team and a team operating system that will take you there.

Leader & Teammate Actions

To ensure your team has a meaningful vision, conduct this simple, three-question, anonymous survey:

1. To what degree do all teammates **understand** the team's vision?
2. To what degree do all teammates **agree** with the team's vision?
3. To what degree do all teammates **actively support** the team's vision?

Compile the results. Then, in a team meeting, invite all teammates to discuss the results.

If the team agrees it needs to refine its vision, assign two teammates to design and facilitate a team workshop to achieve this outcome as soon as it is practical.

Here is a basic structure for creating vision and goals.

Vision is a description of the team's most desirable future. Its purpose is to direct, inspire, and unite. Vision is a statement of:
- purpose, direction, and excellence
- identity and pride
- commitment to achieve 100% customer satisfaction

Business goals are specific steps on the path toward achieving the team vision. They:
- identify specific actions and milestones to be accomplished
- improve product quality, the team operating system, and financial performance

Psychological goals or values are teammate commitments that define how they will *behave while working towards achieving business goals*. These goals and values amplify the worthiness of the vision and naturally motivate teammates.

A Right-Minded Teamwork **Team Operating System** is a 90-day, continuous improvement plan that ensures your team stays focused on achieving 100% customer satisfaction. Your Team Operating System organizes your team processes and procedures. There are six steps in this self-perpetuating process.

 *To Learn More...*

For more, go to RigthMindedTeamwork.com or your favorite book retailer and search for ***Right-Minded Teamwork in Any Team****: The Ultimate Team Building Method to Create a Team That Works as One.*

Your team's ability to achieve its vision, during good times and bad, depends on your teammates' collective willingness to create and follow Work Agreements.

Those who persistently strive to improve teamwork are emotionally mature people who have experienced the deeply gratifying rewards of:

- *renewed trust where there once was suspicion,*
- *restored safety where there once was fear,*
- *revived hope where there once was despair.*

When you and your teammates consciously choose to create and abide by your Work Agreements, you are essentially letting go of your past.

Letting go of the past creates space to strengthen your working relationships as you move forward into the future, which greatly improves your team's ability to resolve conflict and team challenges in the present.

Work Agreements provide clear direction on how your team works as one, doing no harm and getting work done.

Choice #5
Work Agreements:
Bring People Together as One

Bring People Together with Work Agreements

Creating and following Work Agreements is a particularly important characteristic of a successful team. Why? They increase the likelihood that your team will achieve 100% customer satisfaction.

To create Work Agreements, in team-building workshops focused on continuous improvement, teammates openly discuss and agree on work performance behaviors that will clear up unresolved interpersonal or process issues. The issues addressed are either already hurting team performance or have the potential to hurt team performance.

What exactly is a Work Agreement? It is a covenant, promise, or pledge that transforms behaviors. It is not a flimsy ground rule. It is an emotionally mature promise.

Nearly all teamwork topics or issues can be addressed and improved with Work Agreements, of which there are two basic types.

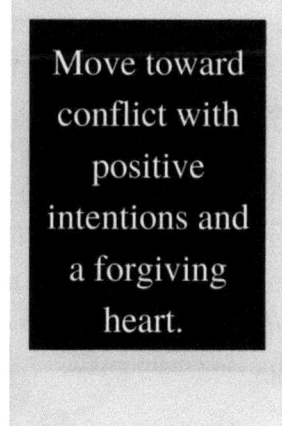

Move toward conflict with positive intentions and a forgiving heart.

A **process** **Work Agreement** describes who will do what and which work methods they will use. These Agreements define work tasks in terms of roles, responsibilities, interfaces, and decision-making.

A **behavioral** **Work Agreement** describes how teammates will behave while they perform their tasks, such as the ways team members will bring to light, communicate, and resolve difficult performance issues or interpersonal conflicts.

A well-written Work Agreement includes an intention statement that defines your team's choice, such as, "Each team member will communicate their thoughts and feelings in appropriate ways."

Each Work Agreement will also have clarification statements such as, "We follow the spirit and intent of our company values. If we believe another person is being inappropriate, we will…" or, "Even though this Agreement describes inappropriate behaviors, we also agree to give positive reinforcement, so we will…"

See Choice #3 for a Communication Work Agreement example.

If you have ever been on any team, you know it is not a matter of whether conflict will occur. It is only a matter of when. For that reason, it is far better to have Work Agreements in place before disagreements occur to mitigate or even make good use of those clashes.

When your team creates and actively lives Right-Minded Work Agreements, you will follow Reason's logic. When Ego attacks happen, and you seek a **moment of Reason**, *your Work Agreements will guide you to recover,* refocusing your collective energy on achieving team goals.

When your team successfully and consistently recovers from challenging situations, you will undoubtedly create and sustain mature working relationships. You will build the kind of relationships that bring teammates together as one.

When you experience a moment of Reason and recover, you will once again be living the quintessential Right-Minded teammate behavior of doing no harm while you work as one.

How do you know you have witnessed a **moment of Reason**? You hear a statement like this that relates to a team's Work Agreements:

"We've already agreed on how to address that issue, haven't we?"

I heard this "moment of Reason" statement in a team's second RMT workshop. When the team realized they had created Work Agreements three months prior that addressed the issue they were re-arguing, they immediately shifted back into their collective Right Mind.

 *To Learn More...*

For the full story, check out the RMT book **How to Facilitate Team Work Agreements**: *A Practical, 10-Step Process for Building a Right-Minded Team That Works as One*. Look for the section "Sustaining Team Work Agreements," and find the portion titled, *"We've already agreed on how we were to address that issue, haven't we?"*

Leader & Teammate Actions

If you and your team are discussing these 9 Right Choices in sequential order, you have already created a Communication Work Agreement (Choice #3). Now it is time to discuss and make any other needed Work Agreements.

Before your next Work Agreement meeting, ask teammates to answer these questions and bring their answers to the meeting.

1. To what degree has the team defined its work processes?
2. To what degree are teammates happy with those work processes?
3. To what degree do teammates believe those work processes will achieve team goals?
4. To what degree do all teammates trust each other?
5. To what degree do all teammates feel safe enough to approach others regarding a problematic relationship issue?
6. To what degree are conflicts resolved in a mutually satisfying manner?
7. To what degree is the team and/or individual members acknowledged and recognized, either inside or outside the team, for a job well done?

For the team meeting itself, there are two parts to the meeting agenda.

1. List and rank-order all the potential teamwork topics that teammates believe would benefit from a Work Agreement.
2. Discuss the most important topic, and create a Work Agreement.

Please stop telling yourself,

"I've got to try harder."

You are already doing that.

*Trying to do everything
only increases the likelihood that
you will make more mistakes.*

*Make the conscious choice to let go
of the many, trivial, low-value tasks.
They harm you and your team.
They stop you from doing no harm
and working as one.*

*Instead, concentrate on the critical few tasks
that will move your team closer
to achieving its vision.*

Choice #6
Critical Few:
Complete Important Tasks First

Clear Your Plate

"Our plates are full. We can't do any more!" Sound familiar?

This is the full-plate syndrome. It is a significant barrier to team performance that is rooted in wrong-minded thinking.

Here is one way to describe how this Ego-driven barrier is created and perpetuated.

A team receives a directive that it must produce more. Teammates pitch in and take on extra work. Fairly soon, some old tasks are not being completed on time.

Pressure is put on the team to complete both the old and the new tasks. People become anxious. They work overtime to try and get it all done. Because of all the added chaos and confusion, tasks take longer to complete.

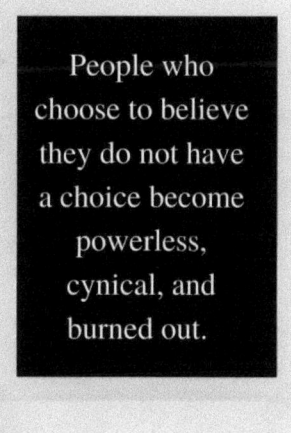

People who choose to believe they do not have a choice become powerless, cynical, and burned out.

Focus and concentration wane. Interpersonal tensions flare. Mistakes are made. Quality suffers. Customers become dissatisfied. Teammates argue.

As a result, a new directive arises for the team to "do it faster, cheaper, and better." In response, the cry of, "We can't do any more!" becomes even louder.

At the root of the full-plate syndrome is the team's collective fear. Your Ego creates and perpetuates this fear by declaring *you will get in trouble if you do not do it all.*

But the truth is you cannot do it all.

Some say, "Yeah, sure. You don't work for our boss. He is happy only when *this* team is continually buzzing with activity, even if it includes low-value tasks. It's the culture around here."

People who choose to believe they do not have a choice become powerless, cynical, and burned out. Rather than realistically prioritizing their workload, they punish themselves. They drain their energy, lose their focus, and make mistakes.

But **Reason** says *you always have a choice.*

You can either win by doing the critical few tasks or lose by attempting to do everything.

Get your team out of the full-plate syndrome. Spend more time doing the right things right, and let go of low-value tasks. Holding on to lower-value tasks is not security. It is incarceration.

Make a case for using your team's vision to identify the critical few tasks. Then, create Work Agreements that channel your energy and resources toward those high-value activities.

Successful teams are those that have learned how to confidently say "no" to tasks that pull them away from their vision, freeing them to do the work that matters most.

When you successfully conduct this exercise, you will mitigate the age-old, flimsy excuse, *"Don't blame me. It's not my job!"*

Leader & Teammate Actions

To encourage the team to choose the critical few, all teammates participate in a roles and responsibilities exercise. The purpose is to ensure teammates are doing the right things right.

During this meeting, expect there to be discussions that evolve into the creation of new Work Agreements.

In preparation, give teammates one to two weeks' notice. Ask teammates to answer these questions and bring their answers to the meeting.

1. What are the two to three *key deliverables*, objectives, or products you produce for the team?

2. What resources or support do you need that you are *currently receiving?*

3. What resources or support do you need that you are *NOT currently receiving?*

4. What are you *getting that you DON'T need?* What is preventing or getting in your way of doing no harm and working as one?

During the meeting, teammates share their answers to these questions.

The **first question** will help you prioritize your team's efforts into high and low-value tasks.

The answers to the **second question** will allow teammates to extend positive regard to one another.

The discussion around the **third question** is about closing responsibility gaps and making new Work Agreements.

And finally, the discussion that follows from the **fourth question** will help the team decide if some tasks do not need to be done any longer.

The outcome of the workshop should be a clear understanding and, in many cases, new teammate Work Agreements.

 *To Learn More...*

For detailed instructions and a guide to help you set up and facilitate this exercise, go to RightMindedTeamwork.com and search for ***Defining Teammate Roles and Responsibilities Using These Four Questions.***

*When team members make a mistake
– and they will, as will you –
correction is called for,
not punishment.*

*The choice to forgive and correct mistakes
is made in your mind.*

*It comes from the Right-Minded Choices
you hold in your heart to forgive,
learn, and move on.*

*Correcting mistakes allows you
to do no harm and work as one.*

Choice #7
Mistakes Happen:
Correct Them; Don't Punish People

Learning Versus Punishment

When teams correct and learn from mistakes, teammates feel safe, and productivity improves.

When people are punished, fear takes over. Little is corrected, mistakes continue, nothing is learned, and productivity declines. This scenario is the opposite of Right-Minded Teamwork's philosophy of "Do no harm. Work as one."

Ample evidence confirms that correcting mistakes is a good business practice. An internet search will quickly reveal many well-known errors that turned out to be huge business successes because they were fixed and leveraged, not blamed or avoided.

Here is a short, mythical story as an example.

There once was an executive who made a multimillion-dollar mistake. The CEO called the executive into his office and purposefully interviewed him. After 10 minutes, the CEO closed the meeting. Confused, the executive began to walk away. Before going far, he turned and said to the CEO, "I thought you were going to fire me." The CEO said, "I just spent millions of dollars on you. Now that I'm convinced you have learned from this mistake, it would be silly to fire you."

When team members go through their workday in fear, they use their energy to defend themselves, depleting their vigor for teamwork.

Unfortunately, feelings of fear, which Ego perpetuates, are pervasive. Fears of:
- being wrong, making mistakes,
- being blamed, not being perfect,
- not knowing where you stand in your relationships, and
- taking risks ... are prime examples.

These fears are easily picked up, reinforced, and blown *far out of proportion* by Ego-driven teammates. When this happens, it can cause negative team comments that distract team members from being fully present and able to perform their duties.

Successful teams follow Reason's advice by creating Work Agreements that spell out how they will correct mistakes. With Reason's guidance, teammates agree to forgive each other, and they embrace the truth that correcting errors is a catalyst for breakthrough learning.

These teammates are, essentially, fearlessly trying new and better ways to achieve their vision because they know they will be safe if honest mistakes happen.

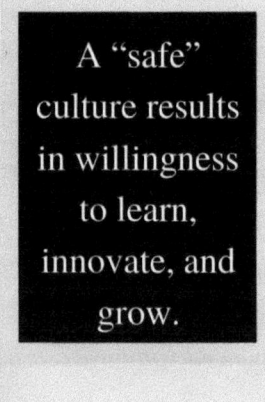

A "safe" culture results in willingness to learn, innovate, and grow.

Their choice is clear: Accept Reason's philosophy that blame is harmful and unhelpful, and correction is essential. Doing this will create a team culture that results in a renewed willingness to learn, risk, change, innovate, and ultimately accomplish more.

Leader & Teammate Actions

All teammates participate in an open discussion that leads to the team creating a Work Agreement describing how teammates will accept, forgive, and resolve mistakes.

If your team is applying all 9 Right Choices, you will also find it beneficial to utilize the 9 Right Choices Survey found in the Resources section of this book. Here is the survey question, or statement, that corresponds to Choice #7. Teammates should reply with yes, no, or maybe:

*We always look for ways to correct mistakes
and improve our team's business performance and relationships.*

When you ask teammates to provide comments on their answers, you will find they provide specific ideas on making your Work Agreements.

Instead of asking this survey question, you can also discuss a recent team mistake as a whole team. If you choose this option, teammates should answer this question:

*If we could do this over again,
what would each of us do differently?*

Regardless of which option you choose, ask teammates to come to the team meeting prepared to offer ideas that will evolve into a Work Agreement.

When you kick off the meeting, begin by asking everyone to let go of their own and others' past mistakes.

Everyone needs to feel safe and believe no one will be blamed for sharing. Once the new Work Agreement is created, the team will be ready to move forward with this new collective mindset.

 ***To Learn More...***

For detailed instructions and a guide to assist you in setting up and facilitating this exercise, go to RightMindedTeamwork.com, and search for ***Utilize the 9 Teammate Questions to Track Your Team's Performance.***

*Demonstrate by your actions,
your behaviors, and your beliefs
that you have risen far above any team situation
that could pull you into Ego's
battleground of conflict.*

*View your team as a classroom,
and you will do no harm and work as one.*

Choice #8
Conflict Happens: Go to the Classroom, Not the Battleground

A Safe Space for Learning

What is so desirable about conflict? It is only caused by Ego's need to be right. Wipe out the desire for battle in your mind.

Instead, rise above any conflicts and battlegrounds happening at work. Transform these challenging situations into learning-focused classrooms. Disputes are going to happen; disagreements are natural. But the benefits of cooperation are far more significant than the spoils of war.

Besides, the conflict itself is often not the actual problem.

The real problem lies in how teammates deal with conflict. If they follow Ego and try to win, they make things worse. But when they follow Reason and open themselves to collaboration, solutions are found.

Creating conflict deliberately is your Ego's advice.

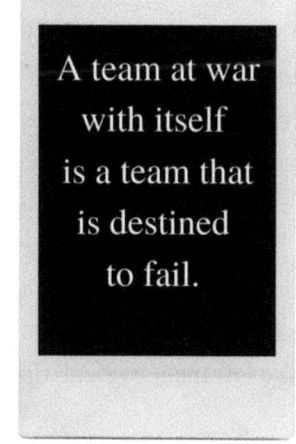
A team at war with itself is a team that is destined to fail.

Reason, on the other hand, encourages you to move kindly toward conflict when it occurs. It tells you to step forward with positive intentions and a forgiving heart.

Once teammates experience the exhilarating energy that comes from resolving conflict, they will wonder why they ever believed in battle.

They will realize that a team at war with itself is a team that is destined to fail.

You can also think about it as if going to your classroom were like going to a playground. Some people, unfortunately, believe they cannot play at work, but this belief is limiting. Learning to incorporate the right level of playfulness in your work classroom can be very empowering.

When you were a child, the playground was a classroom for you. It was a place where you learned about the world. Through play, you found new ways to apply skills such as talking, listening, negotiating, deciding, and exploring.

During play, you accepted mistakes as a natural part of learning. You freely explored new things, feeling safe and supported by your family. When you were a child, you woke up excited to start your day and felt sad to see it end.

Regrettably, too many people have lost touch with the playgrounds in their lives. For them, the world looks far more like a battleground.

For these people, feelings of distrust, competition, survival, fear, anger, and despair have collected inside. Over time, those feelings have left them cynical, distrustful, wounded, and tired.

Here is a true story of warring men who began in battle, experienced a **moment of Reason**, entered their classroom, and, as a result, discovered their playground.

Two men worked in the same department for years. They hated each other so much that when they were physically close, you could feel the distrust.

One day, they begrudgingly attended a team-building exercise.

During a discussion about conflict resolution, one heatedly said to the other, "You never listen to me!" The other replied, "I thought you knew I am hard of hearing. Sometimes I don't know when someone is talking to me."

That single moment of Reason shifted both men from the battleground into the classroom. With that shift, they both began to learn. They continued to talk and found new ways to work together.

In time, they became particularly good co-workers and friends. They even became fishing buddies and enjoyed exploring their new playground together.

Reason continually reminds you that you get to choose whether your team operates in a battleground or a classroom. Do not get drawn into the Ego gossip and relationship wars; rise above those Ego-centric battlegrounds.

No matter what is going on in the rest of the organization, do your part to band teammates together. Your efforts will help to create a Right-Minded classroom environment for your team, and soon you will do no harm and work as one.

Leader & Teammate Actions

All teammates participate in an open discussion that leads to the team creating a conflict resolution Work Agreement. This Agreement should describe how teammates will move into the classroom when conflict happens.

To prepare for the team meeting, ask teammates to answer these questions and bring their answers to the discussion:

1. Where are our team battlegrounds? What behaviors am I seeing? Who is involved?
2. What evidence do I have that shows our team is better off when we resolve our conflicts?
3. Why should I encourage my teammates to learn how to resolve conflicts?
4. What would be the costs if we do not create this Work Agreement?

When you kick off the meeting, begin by asking everyone to let go of their own and others' past conflicts. Everyone needs to feel safe and believe that past conflicts will not be rehashed.

With the new Work Agreement in place, the team will be prepared to deal with conflict productively when it arises.

Everyone wants to be appreciated.

*You want to feel valued.
Accept it. It is perfectly natural.*

*Recognition strengthens your beliefs.
Your beliefs mold your values.
Your values drive your choices.
Your choices propel your behaviors.
Your behaviors produce your results.
Your Right-Minded Teamwork
results warrant recognition.*

Authentic recognition is the means for sustaining your Unified Circle of Right-Minded Thinking.

It is also a smart business decision because recognition is the fuel that powers your Right-Minded Teamwork engine. It plays a critical role in growing your team's business. Forget this, and your team will soon run out of its get-up-and-go.

Implement recognition, and you will always have enough energy to ensure teammates do no harm and work as one.

Choice #9
Recognition:
Make It Easy to Keep Going

Build & Maintain Momentum

Authentic recognition is not about bestowing company shirts and prizes. It is about giving and receiving genuine appreciation for a job well done.

Recognition plays a critical role in growing your team's business because it keeps your team's spirit ignited. It strengthens your team's United Circle of Right-Minded Thinking and, when spirits are high, people stay focused on their jobs. When there is focused concentration, teams tap into an incredible reservoir of innovation.

This innovative power is available to any team that genuinely wants it.

Think about this: What keeps you going in trying times?

Isn't it mostly other people's belief in you that motivates you to keep going?

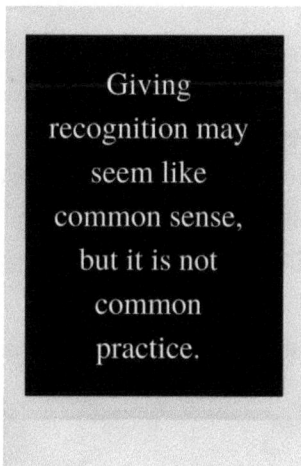

Giving recognition may seem like common sense, but it is not common practice.

You know they believe in you because, in the past, they acknowledged and expressed their authentic appreciation for your legitimate efforts. They recognized you. Remembering their recognition of your past efforts motivated you in the present.

Unfortunately, many people work in team environments where there is little to no recognition.

These teammates are discouraged. They do not give their best to the team. Why should they?

Discouraged teammates are like a racehorse. If he is giving you only 80%, you can whip him, and he will give you 90%. Whip him again, and he will give you 100%.

But if you whip him again, after he has already given you everything he has, he will drop back to 80% or less. He has learned that you are going to whip him regardless, even if he works harder. So why should he give you his best?

Whipped people leave teams. Far too often, the ones who leave are the most talented teammates.

People who receive legitimate and genuine recognition stay and contribute. Shirts and prizes cannot earn that kind of loyalty or effort.

Giving recognition may seem like common sense, but it is not common practice. If it is not practiced in your organization very much, do not get discouraged. Do not let it defeat you, either.

Instead, focus on making sure your teammates recognize one another.

As outsiders see how your team treats each other, they will want to be part of what you have created. As your expressions of appreciation expand to include them, their trust, respect, and collaboration with your team will also grow.

Genuine recognition bonds your teammates and builds feelings of trust, gratitude, and safety. Provide an environment of recognition, and it will help you create and sustain Right-Minded Teamwork.

Leader & Teammate Actions

Facilitate a team discussion about team recognition and individual recognition that will work best for your team.

From that discussion, create a Work Agreement that lists legitimate criteria for giving rewards, including how and when to give recognition.

Ahead of time, ask teammates to answer these questions and bring their answers to the team meeting:

1. Why should my team give authentic recognition?
2. What evidence do I have that shows our team is better off when we give and receive legitimate recognition?
3. Why should I encourage my teammates to create a recognition program?
4. What are the costs and benefits of a recognition program?

When you kick off the team meeting, make sure that all teammates agree the recognition program will be a work-in-progress. That means you will establish a basic plan first with the motto of "start small and fine-tune over time." Capture your decisions in a teammate recognition Work Agreement.

Your New Beginning: You Can Work as One

Your team is your classroom. If you dread going to class, you will never fully understand Right-Minded Teamwork. If you want to be fully functional and emotionally mature, you will gladly embrace your teammates and look forward to attending class every day.

Keep in mind the only freedom you truly have is the freedom to choose how to respond to teamwork challenges. To make the most of your freedom, you must train your mind to apply Reason's Right-Minded choices in good and bad times.

When you align with Reason, Right-Minded work behaviors follow, and your work performance contributes to creating a team that works as one.

The good news is that Right-Minded choices are natural. They are already inside your mind. When you and your teammates are not collaborating or functioning at your best, that is your signal and evidence you are following Ego. Your wrong mind has penetrated your team's thought system. It is time to realign with Reason's Right-Mindedness.

This book does not claim to teach the complete meaning of Right-Mindedness. It is a basic course in Right-Minded Teamwork.

It claims that by discussing and agreeing on how to live these nine, Right-Minded choices in your team, you can remove the blocks to accomplishing Right-Minded Teamwork.

In other words, the fundamental purpose of Right-Minded Teamwork and the 9 Right Choices is to remove the blocks of wrong-minded thinking.

When you do, Reason's Right-Minded truth is revealed to you:

Your team can work as one.

Resources

30 Right-Minded Teamwork Attitudes & Behaviors

Over decades of team-building work, I worked with hundreds of teams. Along the way, I collected their Right-Minded attitudes and behaviors into a list of choices that I grouped into **work behaviors** and **work processes**. Use this list to either adopt or adapt your team's Psychological Goals and Work Agreements.

Was I Born with These Thoughts & Attitudes?

Thoughts and attitudes always precede teamwork behavior.

Right-Minded attitudes come from Reason. Wrong-minded attitudes come from Ego.

The good news is that Right-Minded attitudes are natural. They are already inside you and your teammates.

When you think about any of the wrong-minded Ego attitudes listed below, ask yourself,

> *Was I born with these depressing, debilitating, and awful attitudes?*

Your answer will always be **"no!"** You learned those wrong-minded attitudes from Ego. That means **you can unlearn them, too.**

You Can Change Your Mind

In 35 years of team-building facilitation, I heard too many well-intentioned albeit wrong-minded teammates say,

> *That's just the way I am. I can't change.*

That is **simply not true**.

What is true is that they refused to change their minds.

> *When someone says they cannot change, what they are really saying is their behavior is more powerful than their mind.*

When they realize and joyfully accept that **their mind is in charge**, they have opened the way for happiness, inner peace, and Right-Minded Teamwork.

Why You Want to Change Your Perspective

Fixed perspectives prevent you from achieving Right-Minded Teamwork. Your limiting beliefs, interpretations, and lessons from Ego are blocks to Right-Minded Thinking.

To remove those blocks, you must transform your self-limiting thoughts. The first of RMT's 7 Mindfulness Training Lessons will help you do that.

Lesson one of the 7 Mindfulness Training Lessons states, *"I am never upset for the reason I think."*

Reminding yourself of this truth when you or your teammates are out of your Right mind will help you experience a **moment of Reason**. Instead of seeing your teammate's behavior as a negative Ego attack, you are able to reinterpret their behavior as a desperate **call for help** from you and your teammates.

With this new insight, you are able to respond to your teammate with Reason's wise guidance. With Reason's help, you have effectively changed your perspective.

. . . . .

The 30 Right-Minded Teamwork Attitudes & Behaviors starting on the next page will help you change your perspective and achieve Right-Minded Thinking.

Work Behavior Attitudes

As the Decision-Maker, You Behave One Way or the Other!

EGO — DECISION MAKER — REASON

Demonstrate adversarial competition and power struggles	Demonstrate collaborative competition and synergy
Demonstrate victim or victimizer attitudes & behaviors	Exhibit accountable and responsible attitudes & behavior
Worry that "I am my mistakes;" continue to obsess over mistakes	Embrace that "I am not my mistakes;" mistakes are opportunities for me to learn
Noticeable lack of emotional maturity and empathy	Desire to be emotionally mature and compassionate
Exhibit self-centered attitudes	Exhibit we-centered attitudes
Hold & project grievances; Never forget or forgive	Embrace & extend forgiveness; Let go of issues from the past
After mistakes, helplessness occurs, and I choose to give up or not try as hard	After mistakes, forgiveness occurs, and I choose to try again and again

Work Behavior Attitudes (Continued)

There's a mindset of scarcity, a belief that to give is to lose	There's an attitude of abundance, a belief that to give is to receive
There is suspicion, closed-mindedness, and resistance to change	There is readiness and open-mindedness for positive change
Too often, people restate their position, believing they are right, and others are wrong	We always seek mutual understanding: believing together, we are right
I believe I'm the smartest, and I can prove it	We believe none of us is as smart as all of us
I demonstrate a conscious or unconscious attitude of confusion, chaos, complexity, and drama	We continually demonstrate a conscious attitude of clarity, order, simplicity, and calmness
There's a widespread belief that difficult team situations and changes determine how we feel	We know for sure that our minds determine how we feel about difficult situations or changes
We believe it is best to keep quiet when correction is needed	We have a team culture of appropriately speaking up when a correction is needed
We believe in these attitudes: vulnerability, unkindness, hate, attack, blame	We embrace these attitudes: invulnerability, love, kindness, do no harm, work as one

Work Behavior Attitudes (Continued)

We believe in power over others	We believe in power with others
Growth is painful; remember, if there is no pain, there is no gain	Growth doesn't have to be painful; learning is joyously attained and gladly remembered
It is best to do unto others (reject, attack, defend) before they do unto you	We do unto others (accept, forgive, adjust) as we would have them do unto us
There is a feeling of avoidance and criticism among teammates	There is a spirit of acknowledgment and reward among teammates
There is a love and a need for power, fame, money, and pleasure	We strive for non-attachment to power, fame, money, and pleasure
Our team is a battleground where conflict is prolonged as we act like victims or victimizers	Our team is our learning classroom where conflict is resolved as we act like Right-Minded Teammates
There is mistrust, fear, and lack of safety among teammates	There is trust, peace, and safety among teammates
Defensiveness is prevalent in our team	Defenselessness is widespread in our team

Process Behavior Attitudes

Your Team Can Operate One Way or the Other!

The team's purpose, vision, and mission are unclear and not supported	Our team continuously clarifies our purpose, vision, and mission and actively supports them
There is no discernable team operating system	There is an efficient, continuous improvement team operating system in place
There is a predominant attitude of avoidance and complaining	We have an attitude and a system for acknowledgment and reward
Disagreements and a lack of clear roles and responsibilities exist	We periodically clarify teammate roles and responsibilities
We are unclear who makes decisions and how	Our team has a clear and effective decision-making Work Agreement
We spend too much time and energy applying inefficient work processes	Our work processes and procedures are clear, understood, accepted, and efficient
Too often, people are punished for making mistakes	We always embrace an attitude of converting mistakes into learning opportunities

Actionable Attitudes = Better Behaviors

These Right-Minded attitudes are practical. However, these noble thoughts and attitudes will do no good unless you discuss them and define what they mean for your team.

Once you have identified and defined the behaviors associated with your chosen attitudes, captured in your team Work Agreements, you must also make the conscious choice to live them going forward.

Don't let your team's insignificant, Ego-driven squabbles pull you down.

Be vigilant and demonstrate by your actions and behaviors that you have risen above your old, petty, teamwork battleground issues.

No team situation can pull you into Ego's realm of conflict when you believe it is far better to collaborate and win than argue and lose.

Remember, it is from your collective Right Mind that you create your Work Agreements. And when you make and follow your promises, you are uniting with each other without the Ego. When you do that, you have returned to the United Circle of Right-Minded Thinking. From that unified circle, it will be much easier to recover from any difficult team situation because you have, at that moment, restored your team's collective Right Mind to Reason.

The 10 Characteristics of Right-Minded Teammates

Right-Minded Teammates have diverse backgrounds, vastly different experiences, and display a wide range of skills. No two are alike. Still, there are certain characteristics all Right-Minded Teammates share.

These characteristics align the teammate's authentic self with the RMT motto of *Do no harm and work as one*. They are:

1. Trust
2. Honesty
3. Tolerance
4. Gentleness
5. Joy
6. Defenselessness
7. Generosity
8. Patience
9. Open-mindedness
10. Faithfulness

When you help your team create and live team Work Agreements, they will be well on their way to living these characteristics.

How does the Right-Minded Teammate live these characteristics?

They do two things when difficult situations occur.

First, they remind themselves of their commitment to *thinking* in a do-no-harm way. Second, they choose to demonstrate do-no-harm *behaviors* that align with their Right-Minded attitudes, such as finding solutions to challenging situations.

It is not always easy to do these two things, but it is always that simple.

To encourage your team to embrace and live these Right-Minded characteristics, check out these two RMT books:

7 Mindfulness Training Lessons: Improve Teammates' Ability to Work as One with Right-Minded Thinking will teach you how to apply RMT's seven, powerful thinking lessons to encourage Right-Minded, unified teamwork.

How to Apply the Right Choice Model: Create a Right-Minded Team That Works as One teaches you how to transform a disappointed team customer into a 100% satisfied customer by making Right-Minded choices, all of which align with the above list of characteristics.

For now, though, let's take a closer look at each of these 10, Right-Minded Teammate characteristics.

1. Trust

Trust is the foundational characteristic for teammates who desire to create and sustain Right-Minded Teamwork. Right-Minded Teammates trust one another because their own past experience has taught them that, in all situations, a forgiving attitude creates safety for teammates to collaborate and resolve difficulties.

2. Honesty

For the Right-Minded Teammate, honesty means more than just telling the truth. It refers to consistency in thought and deed. An honest, Right-Minded Teammate is consistently looking within and striving to align thoughts, words, and behaviors with the team's psychological goals and forgiving values. This kind of honesty is essential to creating and sustaining Right-Minded Teamwork.

3. Tolerance

Judgment is the opposite of forgiveness; it implies a lack of trust. Tolerance indicates non-judgment. Tolerant teammates do not judge one another because they know that though they are not the same, all Right-Minded Teammates are equal. Their tolerance creates space for the wisdom of diversity to surface, and their equality allows them to work together as one.

4. Gentleness

Right-Minded Teammates believe that gentleness is the only sane response to challenging situations and circumstances. Whereas harshness and judgment close doors, gentleness opens them. With gentleness, it is easy for teammates to do no harm as they work as one – with teammates and customers alike.

5. Joy

Joy is the inevitable result of Right-Minded teammates who are gentle and non-judgmental. Fear is impossible for those who are gentle, especially during challenging situations. Joy comes from gentleness, tolerance, honesty, and forgiveness.

6. Defenselessness

Right-Minded Teammates understand that defenses are foolish, judgmental attitudes and behaviors that prevent the team from finding solutions to difficult situations. When teammates summon the courage to forgive and trust themselves and to look honestly at their wrong-minded defenses without judgment, they can lay those debilitating arguments gently aside, creating the proper conditions for honestly doing no harm and working as one.

7. Generosity

Right-Minded Teammates honestly and humbly give all they know to help their team create Right-Minded Teamwork and achieve 100% customer satisfaction. The world teaches that if you give something away, you lose it, but Right-Minded Teammates realize that to give *is* to receive. They eagerly participate with their teammates to create solutions to solve challenging situations, bringing joy and satisfaction to the team through their gentle generosity.

8. Patience

Teammates who know Right-Minded Teamwork is the outcome they want can easily afford to wait without concern. Because their goal is to be tolerant and gentle with their teammates, patience comes naturally. The highest desire is to work as one.

9. Open-Mindedness

Judgment, or wrong-mindedness, closes teammates' minds, creating resistance to Right-Minded Teamwork. To ensure they do no harm while working as one, Right-Minded Teammates embrace open-mindedness, also known as Right-Mindedness.

10. Faithfulness

Faithfulness describes a teammate's trust in their team's version of Right-Minded Teamwork. When a teammate is faithful, they effortlessly and wholeheartedly believe in Right-Minded Teamwork. They *want* to do no harm and work as one. They know none of us is as smart as all of us. When applied during challenging circumstances, their faithfulness inevitably leads the team to happy outcomes.

RMT's 9 Right Choices Survey

The 9 Right Choices Survey is a nine-question perception survey. It aligns with the nine choices presented in this book.

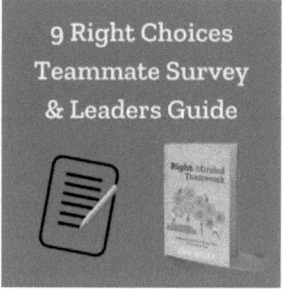

You'll find the survey on the next page, and you may also download it at RightMindedTeamwork.com.

The simplest and fastest way to conduct the survey is in a team meeting, where you'll simply ask team members to complete their questionnaires right then and turn them into the facilitator. When administering the survey, let teammates know everyone will receive a copy of the summary results.

Ask teammates to provide constructive, written comments that help clarify survey scores and make it easier to identify the best outcomes to address in the next workshop.

9 Right Choices Survey

	No 1	2	Yes 3
1. Our team has consciously chosen to follow Reason's Right-Minded choices.			
2. All teammates act and behave as one united team.			
3. All teammates communicate their thoughts, opinions, and ideas in effective and appropriate ways.			
4. All teammates understand, agree, and actively support the team's vision.			
5. Our team has developed creative, effective, and practical work agreements that will help us achieve the team's vision.			
6. Our team focuses on completing the agreed-upon critical-few work processes and does not get drawn into the trivial-many.			
7. We always look for ways to correct mistakes and to improve our team's business performance and relationships.			
8. All conflicts are adequately addressed and resolved in a timely and humanistic manner.			
9. All teammates feel they are appropriately acknowledged & recognized for their job contributions.			
Comments: What should teammates Start, Stop, or Continue doing?			

Analyzing & Using Survey Results

The RMT 9 Right Choices Survey is a "pulse" survey designed to measure the team's collective perception of their current state. It is pretty simple to administer and analyze, making it highly worthwhile.

When you are ready to analyze survey results, there are three tiers of possible performance, no matter your team's size.

If your **Average Team Member's** Score is:

15 or less: Your team is functioning far below potential.

16–22: Your team is doing okay but is still working below potential.

23–27: Your team is doing fine, but you must agree on how to keep it that way.

As for teammate comments, you will want to organize them by creating groups of similar remarks.

If many team members are saying the same thing, you have found a common issue; it is likely a team-building issue to address in the workshop.

Calculating & Summarizing Survey Results

To calculate results, first, tally the scores for each column. Then divide your overall score by the number of teammates to determine the average score.

EXAMPLE: Eight teammates completed the survey.
For question #1, four teammates gave it a 1, three scored 2, and only one person said 3.

Total Team Scores	No 1	2	Yes 3
1. ...follow Right-Minded principles?	4	3	1
2. ...one united team?	3	5	
3. ...communicate in appropriate ways?	2	4	2
4. ...support the team's vision?	3	5	
5. ...practical Work Agreements?	4	2	2
6. ...critical-few work processes?	5	3	
7. ...correct mistakes?	3	4	1
8. ...resolve conflicts?	5	2	1
9. ...recognize job contributions?	5	3	
Subtotal	34	31	7

Calculating the Average Team Member Score

No = 1	34 x 1 =	34
2	31 x 2 =	62
Yes = 3	7 x 3 =	21
	Total numerical score	117
Overall Average Score	117 / 8 =	14.625

The End

Thanks for reading this Right-Minded Teamwork book. If you enjoyed it, wouldn't you please take a moment to leave a review at your favorite retailer or RightMindedTeamwork.com?

In the following pages, you will find something beneficial: a *Glossary of Right-Minded Teamwork Terms and Resources.*

And finally, on behalf of Reason and all the Right-Minded Teammate Decision-Makers, we extend our best wishes to you and your teammates as you create another *Right-Minded Team that Works Together as One.*

Glossary of Right-Minded Teamwork Terms & Resources

100% Customer Satisfaction

Creating 100% customer satisfaction is a primary goal of Right-Minded Teamwork. Your team is responsible for providing quality products and services to customers; for your team and enterprise to succeed, your customers deserve to be 100% satisfied.

With a strong customer satisfaction plan, as described in *Right-Minded Teamwork in Any Team*, your teammates will strive to achieve customer satisfaction while consistently achieving other business goals.

7 Mindfulness Training Lessons

Achieving Right-Minded Teamwork involves adopting an attitude of mindfulness. The *7 Mindfulness Training Lessons* teach you to think in a Right-Minded way, ensuring you **do no harm** as you **work as one** with your teammates.

These powerful lessons are summed up in one sentence, with emphasis on three words:

*Right-Minded Teammates **accept**, **forgive**, and **adjust** their thinking and work behavior.*

In every circumstance, especially during difficult team situations, Right-Minded Teammates practice mindfulness to move them from defensiveness and blame into a Right-Minded, allied way of thinking and behaving.

Inspired by *A Course in Miracles* and our Right Choice Model, the *7 Mindfulness Training Lessons* is a teaching tool designed to help those willing to apply them to ensure they return to the Unified Circle of Right-Minded Thinking.

Go to RightMindedTeamwork.com or visit your favorite book retailer to pick up your copy of **7 Mindfulness Training Lessons**: *Improve Teammates' Ability to Work as One with Right-Minded Thinking.*

10 Characteristics of Right-Minded Teammates

Right-Minded Teammates have many different surface traits and personalities. They are not all alike. They have numerous backgrounds, vastly different experiences, and a wide range of skills.

Nevertheless, it is understood that the Right-Minded Teammate, in their own particular behavioral style, happily live these characteristics because they align the teammate's authentic *self* with their team's version of the RMT motto: *do no harm, work as one,* and *none of us is as smart as all of us.*

You will find a complete description of these characteristics in RMT's book: ***Right-Minded Teamwork in Any Team: The Ultimate Team Building Method to Create a Team That Works as One.***

1. Trust	2. Honesty	3. Tolerance
4. Gentleness	5. Joy	6. Defenselessness
7. Generosity	8. Patience	9. Open-Mindedness
	10. Faithfulness	

12 Steps Workshop Design Process

Design a Right-Minded, Team-Building Workshop: 12 Steps to Create a Team That Works as One. This book will teach you how to design a practical, real-world team-building workshop.

The 12 steps are grouped into three phases: Contract, Commence, and Carry on. Written primarily for team facilitators, team leaders, and teammates can easily follow the steps to design a successful team-building workshop. Because this method engages teammates in designing the agenda, it virtually guarantees that teammates *cannot wait* to attend the workshop. They *know* that they will get real work done in a safe, "no harm" environment when they meet.

A Course in Miracles

Oneness. Forgiveness is the key to happiness, inner peace, undifferentiated unity, and ultimately – *Oneness*. "A Course In Miracles (ACIM) is a unique spiritual self-study program designed to awaken us to the truth of our *Oneness* with God and Love," as posted on ACIM.org and ACIM.org/ACIM/en. See the Foundation for A Course in Miracles at FACIM.org, where Ken Wapnick, the founder, created this beautiful definition.

> *A Course in Miracles is a psychological approach to spirituality where forgiveness is the central theme, and inner peace is the result.*

ACIM and other moral and spiritual philosophies that advocate and help people everywhere **work together as One** has inspired Right-Minded Teamwork. We used Ken's definition as a guide to create the Right-Minded Teamwork definition.

> *Right-Minded Teamwork is a business-oriented, psychological approach to team building where acceptance, forgiveness, and adjustments are teammate characteristics, and 100% customer satisfaction is the team's result.*

All Right-Minded Teamwork methods, processes, and tools seamlessly work together to help you create and sustain a *Team That Works Together as* ***One****.*

Accept, Forgive, Adjust

These three terms are at the core of Right-Minded Teammate Attitudes & Behaviors. These verbs are also central to the *7 Mindfulness Training Lessons*, which are summed up in the sentence, *Right-Minded Teammates* **accept**, **forgive**, *and* **adjust** *their thinking and work behavior.*

Furthermore, these three concepts are included in the definition of Right-Minded Teamwork:

> *Right-Minded Teamwork is a business-oriented, psychological approach to team building where **acceptance**, **forgiveness**, and **adjustment** are teammate characteristics, and 100% customer satisfaction is the team's result.*

Lastly, these terms are also incorporated as three of the five steps in the *Right Choice Model*, which describes accountable and responsible Right-Minded Teamwork behavior.

Ally or Adversary Teammate

Right-Minded Teamwork asserts that as teammates, you either work together as allies or pull apart, viewing each other as adversaries.

Allies work towards achieving team goals. Adversaries work towards individual elevation, which separates and divides the team.

To determine whether you are in an ally or adversary mindset, ask yourself, *Do I want to be right, or do I want our team to be successful?* Allies want to be part of a successful team. Adversaries want to be right, no matter the cost.

As an adversary, Ego persuades you to compete with your teammates. As an ally, Reason says the opposite. Reason gently reminds you that separateness prevents true success. There cannot be Oneness or collaboration where there is competition.

As the Decision-Maker, you choose to follow either Reason or Ego. You either collaborate or compete. You are an ally or adversary. There is no middle ground.

If you choose to follow Reason and become an ally, you embrace and live your team's Work Agreements. If you decide to follow Ego, you become an adversary, creating a battleground inside yourself and your team.

To transform competitive adversaries into collaborative allies, start by following the *Right Choice Model*, creating team *Work Agreements*, and applying the *7 Mindfulness Training Lessons*.

Avoidance Behavior

Even though the term "avoidance behavior" is not often mentioned in the Right-Minded Teamwork model or books, avoidance behavior is easy to detect in teammates and RMT processes. If you notice it occurring, from an RMT perspective, you can consider it wrong-minded, adversarial behavior.

Identifying avoidance behaviors and attitudes and understanding the harm they cause is the first step in moving from a wrong-minded place into Right-Mindedness. The *7 Mindfulness Training Lessons* and the *Right Choice Model* are excellent tools for teaching yourself and your team how to act and behave in a Right-Minded, accountable way.

For example, if you look carefully at the *Right Choice Model's* lower loop, you will notice that the victim or victimizer first avoids the situation when a difficult situation occurs.

When Right-Minded Teammates ask themselves the *Right Choice Model* question, *How did I create, promote, or allow this difficult situation to happen?* they often realize they have unconsciously demonstrated avoidance behavior. Then, noticing their mistake, they simply choose to **accept**, **forgive**, and **adjust** their approach and return to living in accordance with their team *Work Agreements*.

Battleground:
Where People Are Punished for Mistakes

The battleground represents wrong-minded thinking. It is a mental attitude or thought system that defends and encourages adversarial behaviors such as blame and attack.

Think of the battleground as a psychological symbol for those moments when you realize you are listening to Ego, not Reason (like when you notice avoidance behavior). You recognize that you are having an Ego attack for whatever reason and have made a wrong-minded choice. When you are in the battleground, you "punish" others for their mistakes, either by victimizing others or becoming a victim yourself.

On the other hand, when you are in your Right Mind, you see your team as a lovely and safe classroom, the opposite of the battleground. You do not punish others. You choose, instead, to rise above the conflict.

The purpose of recognizing the battlegrounds in your mind is to own the pain that you are causing yourself which helps you recognize that you consciously want to leave it, overlook it, rise above it, and to transport your mind into the classroom where you return to the forgiving Unified Circle of Right-Minded Thinking with your teammates.

Right-Minded Teammates working in safe and supportive classrooms do not fight, blame, or punish. Instead, they choose Oneness over separateness. They are committed to the team's success and achieving team goals.

To overcome a battleground in yourself or your team, go to RightMindedTeamwork.com, or visit your favorite book retailer to pick up your copy of *How to Apply the Right Choice Model: Create a Right-Minded Team That Works as One*. Inside, you will find a list of battleground attitudes and behaviors as well as the costs and benefits of classroom versus battleground thinking and behaving.

Certified Master Facilitator (CMF)

The Certified Master Facilitator (CMF) credential is a mark of excellence for facilitators. It is the highest available certification for facilitators. To learn more or to find a certified facilitator worldwide, visit the International Institute for Facilitation at INIFAC.org.

Classroom:
Where People Learn from Mistakes

Like the battleground, the classroom is a symbol. But unlike the battlefield, where people punish or are punished, the classroom is where you learn and find inspiration.

At some point in your past, you have experienced the joy and wonder of learning. Right-Minded Teamwork invites you to view your team as a safe place to experience this wonder and joy as you learn new teamwork skills and collaborate to achieve team goals.

When you are experiencing fear in any form or realize you are having an Ego attack, you are in the battleground. To return to the classroom, say to yourself, *There is nothing to fear. In my mind, I choose to rise above this silly battleground and head to my Right-Minded classroom. There, we are committed to do no harm and work as one. There, we will find solutions.*

By recognizing the fear behind your Ego attack and reminding yourself to return to the classroom, you experience a **moment of Reason**. You also strengthen your Right-Minded thought system and restore yourself to Right-Minded Thinking.

In the RMT book *How to Apply the Right Choice Model: Create a Right-Minded Team That Works as One,* you will find a list of 30 Right-Minded and wrong-minded attitudes and behaviors, plus the associated costs and benefits to your team.

Communication Work Agreement

What you think – *your thought system* – drives your communication in one of two ways. You either communicate as a collaborative ally or as a competitive, dysfunctional, and emotionally immature adversary.

Teams that work as one and achieve their goals regularly seek out opportunities to improve communication. They take positive action by creating and living a Communication Work Agreement that describes their team's agreed-upon communication style.

Right-Minded communication is a core concept in the book ***Right-Minded Teamwork: 9 Right Choices for Building a Team That Works as One,*** available at RightMindedTeamwork.com or your favorite book retailer.

To create your team's Communication Work Agreement, follow the suggestions in the book ***How to Facilitate Teamwork Agreements: A Practical, 10-Step Process for Building a Right-Minded Team That Works as One.***

In there, you will find two real examples of which one is a team Communication Work Agreement.

Create, Promote, Allow

These three concepts form the foundation of the *Right Choice Model's* essential question:

*How have I **created, promoted**, or **allowed** this situation to occur?*

Asking and honestly answering this question ensures teammates are "owning their part" in a difficult situation.

These three concepts are also integrated into *7 **Mindful Training Lessons**: Improve Teammate's Ability to Work as One with Right-Minded Thinking.*

High-performing Right-Minded Teammates always ask themselves this question because it leads them to solutions. It is a clear demonstration of the RMT motto, "**Do no harm. Work as one.**"

Critical Few: Complete Important Tasks First

When a team is stuck in the "full-plate syndrome," identifying and completing the critical few - those tasks that have the largest and most direct impact on the team's success - is key to moving forward.

At the root of the full-plate syndrome is the **team's collective fear**, driven by Ego, which declares you will get in trouble if you do not do it all… even though the truth is you can never do it all.

People who listen to Ego believe they do not have a choice. Rather than realistically prioritizing their workload, they punish themselves for failing to meet the unreasonable goal of completing everything. They drain their energy, lose their focus, and make mistakes. They become powerless, cynical, and burned out.

But Reason reminds us that we always have this choice:

We can either win by doing the critical few tasks, or we can lose by attempting to do everything.

Spend more time doing the right things right and let go of low-value tasks. Holding on to lower-value tasks is **not security**. It is **incarceration**.

The "critical few" concept is discussed in the book *Right-Minded Teamwork: 9 Right Choices for Building a Team That Works as One*.

See **Recognition: Make It Easy to Keep Going** for a related concept.

Decision-Maker: The Real You

Ken Wapnick, Ph.D., created the term "Decision-Maker" to define the "real you" in *A Course in Miracles*. For more on his work, visit FACIM.org.

Within Right-Minded Teamwork, the *Right Choice Model* uses the term "Decision-Maker" to describe the part of you that chooses to listen to and follow either the wrong-minded ways of Ego or the Right-Minded ways of Reason.

Your Decision-Maker is 100% responsible for who you choose to follow, what you choose to think, and how you choose to behave.

Right-Mindedness is achieved when you listen to and follow Reason. Listening means calming your Ego mind, trusting your intuition, and allowing space for a **moment of Reason** to arise.

When Right-Mindedness becomes an integral part of a team, the team consistently works together as one, doing no harm, within the forgiving Unified Circle of Right-Minded Thinking. When teammates do that, they are demonstrating and extending Right-Minded Teamwork to everyone.

To learn more about Reason, Ego, and the Decision-Maker, pick up the book ***Reason, Ego, & the Right-Minded Teamwork Myth****: The Philosophy & Process for Creating a Right-Minded Team That Works Together as One*.

Decision-Maker: Trust Your Intuition

If thinking about Reason and Ego is new to you, it can be helpful to think of Reason as your positive intuition and Ego as your negative, arrogant, and sometimes vindictive intuition.

At different times throughout our lives, we all have listened to and followed each of these teachers.

Stop and remember when you had a hunch or a feeling as to what you should do or say in a particular situation. Did you ignore your intuition? Let's say you did not follow your instinct, and it turned out to be a mistake. What did you say to yourself and others?

> *I wish I had trusted my intuition!*

As this memory illustrates, **you already know how to listen and be mindful** of your intuition. It is your natural, pre-separation state of mind [See **Oneness vs. Separateness**].

You just need to do it regularly.

Decision-Making Work Agreement

Every team needs a Decision-Making Work Agreement that clearly defines how decisions are made and who makes them. Creating a general agreement and putting it into your team's Operating System's Business Plan as a team Work Agreement makes good business sense.

If you do not currently have a Decision-Making team agreement or you have not updated it recently, I highly recommend you do that as soon as it is practical.

Incidentally, Decision-Making is #18 in the *Team Performance Factor Assessment* that you will use every 90 days to keep your team focused and on track. See **Team Operating System**.

In the book, ***How to Facilitate Team Work Agreements**: A Practical, 10-Step Process for Building a Right-Minded Team That Works as One,* you will find two real agreement examples. The first one is a behavioral team Communication Work Agreement, and the other is a Decision-Making Work Agreement. Check it out and use it as a model for your team's Decision-Making Work Agreement.

Desire & Willingness:
Preconditions for Accountability

Even though the terms "desire" and "willingness" are not often mentioned in Right-Minded Teamwork materials (except within the *Right Choice Model*), Right-Mindedness and accountability are virtually synonymous.

The concepts of desire and willingness permeate all RMT methods and processes simply because it is impossible to think in a Right-Minded way, behave with Right-Minded Accountability, and achieve Right-Minded Teamwork without a heartfelt desire and genuine willingness to do so.

The Right Choice Model found in the book *How to Apply the Right Choice Model: Create a Right-Minded Team That Works as One* teaches that *Right-Minded accountability is the desire and willingness to change my mind and behavior in order to effectively respond to difficult team situations.*

If you share the Right Choice Model with your team and distribute the Right Choice cards to teammates, you will see the definition of "desire and willingness" on the cards.

Do No Harm. Work as One.

The Right-Minded philosophy is founded on two universal truths:

*Do No Harm.
Work As One.*®

None of us is as smart as all of us.
Right-Minded Teammates know that working collaboratively together, in a Right-Minded manner, is the only way to create the kind of teamwork that achieves and sustains 100% customer satisfaction. Said differently, these teammates genuinely want and need their fellow teammates.

Do no harm and work as one.
As a Right-Minded Teammate, you can be firm, direct, gentle, and compassionate, all at the same time. You do not blame yourself or others for mistakes. You and your teammates are allies, not adversaries, working together towards your shared goals.

Ego & Ego Attack

Ego is the negative, wrong-minded teacher who continually tells you how difficult the world is and how you must constantly fight to survive.

Reason is the opposite of Ego. Reason teaches you to *do unto others as you would have them do unto you.*

Ego believes everyone is out to get you and directs you to *do unto others before they do unto you.* Ego is also the creator of the tiny, mad idea of separation presented in the *Right-Minded Teamwork Myth*.

An Ego attack is a flash of negative, out-of-control emotion. It happens when you believe the awful feeling you are experiencing has been caused by something someone else said or did to you. Without thinking, you become behaviorally triggered; your body language, tone of voice, and the words you say become mean-spirited. An Ego attack is the opposite of a **moment of Reason**.

As soon as you realize you are experiencing an Ego attack, you must train your mind to say, *I am angry. I have lost control. I'm not upset for the reason I think. I am out of my right mind. I need a moment of Reason to gain control of my attitude. I must return to the classroom so I can find a Right-Minded way of replying that allows us to do no harm and work as one.*

Interlocking Accountability

Interlocking accountability is a crucial RMT concept that is primarily used in *How to Facilitate Team Work Agreements: a Practical, 10-Step Process for Building a Right-Minded Team That Works as One.*

When your team creates Work Agreements, it is highly recommended that one of your agreements includes an interlocking accountability statement so that teammates agree, ahead of time, how to compassionately confront a teammate who continues to break your Work Agreements.

Interlocking accountability means many things, including:

- Giving positive reinforcement when someone continues to do a great job of living the Work Agreements.
- Confronting someone in a supportive and safe but firm way if they continue to break the spirit or letter of the team's Work Agreement.
- Being accountable to each other for achieving or accomplishing the desired outcome of the Work Agreements.
- Recovering and learning from mistakes rather than denying or punishing those who make mistakes. This strengthens team spirit and trust.
- Creating and sustaining teammate trust because teammates who believe everyone will live their part of the Work Agreement will create Right-Minded Teamwork.

Moment of Reason

When you are facing a challenge such as an Ego attack, and you experience a positive and perhaps surprising moment of revelation, clarity, or sanity, you have achieved a moment of Reason.

These moments occur when you genuinely try to move from the battleground into the classroom. When Reason's teaching breaks through, you move from wrong-mindedness into Right-Mindedness.

Moments of Reason are magnificent. They are a cornerstone of your Right-Minded thought system. When they happen, you feel confident and at peace. You know what you should do, what to say, and to whom.

In moments of Reason, you know beyond a shadow of a doubt that you want and need your teammates. You easily return to the Unified Circle of Right-Minded Thinking, where teammates forgive one another, do no harm, and work as one.

Onboarding New Teammates

When a new leader or teammate joins your team, it is vitally important to properly onboard them within their first week on the job. In a single short meeting where everyone attends, the onboarding is easily and effectively accomplished.

Present all your RMT goals and Work Agreements along with why they were created. They ask you clarifying questions. Afterward, you ask them to accept the team's goals and actively live the team's Work Agreements.

Oneness vs. Separateness

Oneness is a psychological state of mind. It can be described in many ways using phrases such as *None of us is as smart as all of us,* or *do no harm,* and *work as one.*

Separateness is the opposite of Oneness. To become a Right-Minded teammate, you must train your mind to choose attitudes and behaviors that create and extend Oneness, not project separateness.

For a list of 30 examples of Oneness, see the Right-Minded Teamwork Attitudes & Behaviors list found in numerous RMT books.

The concepts and story behind Oneness and separateness are introduced in RMT's book, **Reason, Ego & the Right-Minded Teamwork Myth:** *The Philosophy and Process for Creating a Right-Minded Team That Works Together as One.*

In this book, you will learn about Ego's "tiny, mad idea" of wanting more "stuff" and how Ego's choices led us all into a world of separation. That tiny, mad moment was, literally, the **birth of separation**. But, as the Myth reveals, Reason is always ready to lead us back into Oneness - our pre-separation state – joyfully described as the Unified Circle of Right-Minded Thinking where we can do no harm and work as one.

Preventions & Interventions

In RMT's *Design a Right-Minded, Team-Building Workshop: 12 Steps to Create a Team That Works as One*, the team-building facilitator and team leader meet early on to proactively identify potential issues that could keep teammates from achieving the workshop's desired outcomes.

This discussion leads to creating *preventions* that the team leader or facilitator takes to help prevent those issues from happening. The facilitator and team leader also agree on how to intervene in case the preventions don't work. Much of the time, however, preventions do their job and make *interventions* during team-building workshops unnecessary.

To learn more about effective preventions and interventions, go to RightMindedTeamwork.com or your favorite book retailer, and pick up your copy of these two books:

How to Facilitate Team Work Agreements: *A Practical, 10-Step Process for Building a Right-Minded Team That Works as One*

Design a Right-Minded, Team-Building Workshop: *12 Steps to Create a Team That Works as One*

Psychological Goals

A team's psychological goals describe how teammates intentionally choose to think and behave as they work together to achieve their team's business goals.

Psychological goals, such as achieving mutual trust and respect among teammates, may be viewed as a team's collective school of thought, values, or thought system.

These consciously chosen goals, captured in team Work Agreements, clarify the team's principles or standards of behavior.

Here is a specific example of a psychological goal you will find in several RMT materials:

> *When difficult team situations happen, we accept, forgive, and adjust our attitudes and behavior. We always find solutions because we believe that none of us is as smart as all of us.*

Reason

Reason is a mythological character and symbolic guide who shows you how to think and behave in a Right-Minded way. As your Right-Minded teacher, Reason helps you differentiate and choose between Right-Minded and wrong-minded attitudes and behaviors.

Reason is the opposite of Ego. Whereas Ego believes everyone is out to get you and instructs you to *do unto others before they do unto you,* Reason teaches you to *do unto others as you would have them do unto you.*

Ego encourages and projects separateness.
Reason cultivates and extends Oneness.

Reason is that part of your mind that always speaks for the Right Choice attitudes and behaviors. When you need a **moment of Reason** to find the best way to respond to a difficult team situation, say to yourself:

> *I am here to be truly helpful.*
>
> *I am here to represent Reason who sent me.*
>
> *I do not have to worry about what to say or what to do because Reason who sent me will direct me.*

When you experience a moment of Reason (a moment of revelation, clarity, or sanity regarding a particular challenge), "remembering" Reason's gentle guidance towards Oneness restores your mind to the forgiving Unified Circle of Right-Minded Thinking.

For the full story of Ego's tiny, mad idea of separation and how Reason waits even today to bring us back to Oneness, pick up a copy of *Reason, Ego & the Right-Minded Teamwork Myth: The Philosophy and Process for Creating a Right-Minded Team That Works Together as One.*

Reason, Ego & the Right-Minded Teamwork Myth

This book teaches two significant concepts:

- the Right-Minded Teamwork Myth, a short tale that presents RMT's underlying teamwork philosophy of doing no harm and working as one
- the Right-Minded Teamwork team-building tools, methods, and processes to create Right-Minded, productive teams.

The RMT Myth is a short, simple story. It follows three characters: Reason, Ego, and you, the Decision-Maker. Simply put, the RMT Myth and philosophy advocate for teammates to follow Reason's path of Oneness instead of following the Ego's disastrous advice to seek separateness and prioritize selfishness.

Following the RMT Myth, you will learn about the Right-Minded Teamwork process. Unlike the story, the RMT process is no myth. It is practical, deliberate, and reliable.

The RMT process is a set of interconnected, team-building methods that together form a self-perpetuating, continuous improvement system. This process allows you to integrate the aspirations of the RMT Myth into your team in a way that helps you achieve your business goals.

This book teaches the RMT process and provides a clear overview of the seven other RMT team-building books that, when used together, form a continuous improvement process guaranteed to support team growth and success.

Recognition: Make It Easy to Keep Going

Authentic recognition is not about bestowing company shirts and prizes. It is about giving and receiving genuine appreciation for a job well done.

Recognition plays a critical role in growing your team's business because it keeps your team's spirit ignited. Unfortunately, many people work in team environments where there is little to no recognition. These teammates are discouraged. They do not give their best to the team. Why should they?

Discouraged teammates are like racehorses. If a horse is giving you only 80%, you can whip him, and he will give you 90%. Whip him again, and he will give you 100%. But if you whip him again, after he has already given you everything he has, he will drop back to 80%, or maybe even less. He has learned that you are going to whip him regardless, even if he works harder. So why should he give you his best?

Whipped people leave teams.

Far too often, the ones who leave are the most talented teammates. People who receive legitimate and genuine recognition stay and contribute. Shirts and prizes cannot earn that kind of loyalty or effort.

RIGHT-MINDED TEAMWORK: 9 RIGHT CHOICES · 153

In the book *Right-Minded Teamwork: 9 Right Choices for Building a Team That Works as One*, you will learn that Recognition is one of the 9 Right Choices.

See **Critical Few: Complete Important Tasks First** for a related concept.

Right Choice Model

The *Right Choice Model* is an effective teaching aid that will help you and your teammates choose your own set of unique, "right" teamwork attitudes and behaviors.

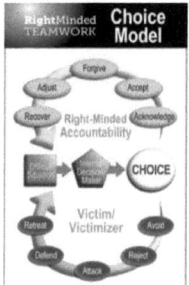

Inspired by *A Course in Miracles*, *The Right Choice Model* consists of two circles. The upper loop of acceptance, forgiveness, and adjustment represents the Unified Circle of Right-Minded Thinking.

The lower loop of rejection, Ego attack, and defensiveness describes the separated or divided circle of wrong-minded thinking.

To learn more about this simple but powerful teaching model, go to RightMindedTeamwork.com or your favorite book retailer, and pick up your copy of *How to Apply the Right Choice Model: Create a Right-Minded Team That Works as One*.

Right-Minded Teamwork's 5-Element Framework

Right-Minded Teamwork is a business-oriented, psychological approach to team building where acceptance, forgiveness, and adjustment are teammate characteristics, and 100% customer satisfaction is the team's result.

Right-Minded Teamwork is built off a framework of 5 Elements consisting of two goals and three teamwork methods.

1. Team **Business Goal**: Achieve 100% Customer Satisfaction
2. Team **Psychological Goal**: Commit to Right-Minded Thinking
3. Team **Work Agreements**: Create & Follow Commitments
4. **Team Operating System**: Make It Effective & Efficient
5. **Right-Minded Teammates**: Strengthen Individual Performance

To learn more, go to RightMindedTeamwork.com or your favorite book retailer, and pick up your copy of ***Right-Minded Teamwork in Any Team****: The Ultimate Team-Building Method to Create a Team That Works as One*.

Right-Minded Teamwork's 5 Element Implementation Plan

There is no one right way to implement RMT's 5 Elements but the three-workshop plan presented in the book *Right-Minded Teamwork in Any Team: The Ultimate Team-Building Method to Create a Team That Works as One* has proven effective countless times.

Here's a brief overview.

First Workshop
Create **psychological goals** plus at least one **Work Agreement**.

Second Workshop
Reaffirm **business goals** and agree on a **team operating system**.

Third Workshop
Encourage and support Right-Minded **Teammate development**.

After the third workshop, and every 90 days after that, you will apply RMT's *Team Operating System & Performance Factor Assessment* to identify opportunities, take action, and achieve new teamwork improvements.

Right-Minded Teamwork Attitudes & Behaviors

The Right-Minded Teamwork model includes a list of 30 behavioral and process-oriented teammate attitudes and behaviors with their associated costs and benefits. I collected and compiled these over three decades of team-building workshops.

This valuable list includes clear, specific, right, and wrong behaviors "taught" to us by either Reason or Ego.

Thoughts and attitudes always precede teamwork behavior. Right-Minded attitudes come from Reason. Wrong-minded attitudes come from Ego.

The good news is that Right-Minded attitudes are natural. They are already inside you and your teammates. When you think about any of the wrong-minded Ego attitudes listed you will see in the list, ask yourself,

> *Was I born with these depressing, debilitating, and awful attitudes?*

Your answer will always be **"no!"** You learned those wrong-minded attitudes from Ego. That means *you can unlearn them, too*.

You can find the list in several RMT books, including ***How to Apply the Right Choice Model***: *Create a Right-Minded Team That Works as One*, available at RightMindedTeamwork.com or your favorite book retailer.

Right-Mindedness vs. Wrong-Mindedness

"Mindedness" is what you choose to think and perceive. Right-Mindedness refers to the positive mental state, perceptions, choices, and actions you demonstrate when following Reason's guidance.

Wrong-mindedness refers to the negative mental state that occurs when you follow Ego's advice.

> *Mindfulness is a journey without distance to a goal you want to achieve.*

In the book *How to Apply the Right Choice Model: Create a Right-Minded Team That Works as One*, you will find a list of rewards and consequences for choosing Right-Mindedness.

In the book *7 Mindfulness Training Lessons: Improve Teammates' Ability to Work as One with Right-Minded Thinking*, you will learn that in every circumstance, and especially during difficult team situations, Right-Minded Teammates practice mindfulness, or Right-Mindedness, to move them into an ally-focused way of thinking and behaving.

Both of these books will help you accept that your mind is split between two thought systems. At one moment, you are following Reason, and the next, Ego. It is impossible to create and sustain Right-Minded Thinking with a split mind. To heal your split mind, you want to apply the *7 Mindful Training Lessons* and the *Right Choice Model's* attitudes and behaviors.

To bring your team back into the forgiving Unified Circle of Right-Minded Thinking, pick up your copy of these books at your favorite book retailer or RightMindedTeamwork.com.

RMT Facilitator

The RMT Facilitator has a special function. Simply put, their expert facilitation *transforms* well-meaning dysfunctional souls into *healthy and functional teammates*.

Using the array of RMT tools, the RMT Facilitator guides teammates in converting their team mistakes into *do-no-harm-work-as-one* attitudes and behaviors.

Teammates are perpetually grateful for the RMT facilitator's help in achieving and sustaining Right-Minded Teamwork. Some even say their RMT Facilitator *saved them*. Team leaders and teammates continually seek the RMT Facilitator's support for years to come.

Team transformations are the RMT Facilitator's **special function**.

Team Management System:
An RMT Enterprise-Wide Process

An enterprise's Team Management System (TMS) aligns all teammates' attitudes and work behavior throughout the organization. An effective TMS ensures everyone is doing their part to help the organization achieve the enterprise's vision, mission, and strategic goals.

RMT's Team Management System involves integrating RMT's 5-Element Framework into all teams.

1. Team **Business Goal**: Achieve 100% Customer Satisfaction
2. Team **Psychological Goal**: Commit to Right-Minded Thinking
3. Team **Work Agreements**: Create & Follow Commitments
4. **Team Operating System**: Make It Effective & Efficient
5. **Right-Minded Teammates**: Strengthen Individual Performance

To learn more, go to RightMindedTeamwork.com or your favorite book retailer, and purchase your copy of *Achieve Your Organization's Strategic Plan: Create a Right-Minded, Team Management System to Ensure All Teams Work as One.*

Team Operating System & Performance Factor Assessment

RMT's Team Operating System is a six-step, 90-day, continuous improvement operating system that organizes your team functions to increase the likelihood of achieving customer satisfaction.

The system also includes the *Team Performance Factor Assessment* [step 3], which you will use to help teammates identify two to three improvement opportunities every 90 days.

The 25 performance factors in this assessment are aligned with and thus measure the six steps of RMT's Team Operating System. They effectively measure all aspects of Right-Minded Teamwork.

If you want your team to operate more effectively and efficiently, apply this 90-day process after your team has completed the first three RMT workshops. For a brief explanation, see the glossary: *Right-Minded Teamwork's 5 Element Implementation Plan*.

Apply the three-workshop plan and the operating system, and you nearly guarantee your team will create Right-Minded Teamwork.

To learn the process, go to RightMindedTeamwork.com or your favorite book retailer, and pick up your copy of **Right-Minded Teamwork in Any Team:** *The Ultimate Team-Building Method to Create a Team That Works as One.*

Thought System

<u>What you believe *is* your thought system</u>. Pause and reflect on this truth, and above all, be thankful that it is true.

Whether you are consciously aware of it or not, your thought system is the lens through which you view the world. Without exception, everyone has one. And though there are many variations, there are **only two thought systems** from which to choose:

- A Right-Minded thought system, which extends ally beliefs of acceptance, forgiveness, and adjustment to everyone, everywhere, forever
- A wrong-minded system, which projects adversarial assaults of rejection, attack, and defensiveness to everyone, everywhere, forever

Once you have developed a thought system of any kind, you live it and teach it. Even if you are not entirely aware of it, it remains at the forefront of your mind, influencing your daily behaviors and choices.

If your thought system is negative, or you choose to follow Ego into an unnecessary and adversarial competition, you cannot be a happy, successful teammate.

To live in the land of Oneness where your workplace is a safe and supportive classroom and where you and your teammates work as one to achieve team goals, you must train your mind and align your thought system with the teachings of Reason.

There is no possible compromise between these two thought systems. You either collaborate, or you compete. When you follow Ego, you take your team to the battleground. When you choose to follow Reason, you willingly create and genuinely strive to live your team's Work Agreements. With Reason's help, you transform your team into a lovely, collaborative, successful classroom.

The choice is clear.

Reject Ego. Embrace Reason.

Be Thankful.

Train Your Mind

When your mind is well-trained in Reason's Decision-Making ways, Ego attacks do not throw you off course. When a difficult team situation happens, you immediately stop for a **moment of Reason**. You refocus on Oneness, rise above the battleground, and remember to live your Work Agreements in your classroom.

To train your mind simply means practicing your team's Work Agreements, which represent your psychological goals, as often as possible, especially during difficult team situations.

Uncovering Root Cause

The Right-Minded Teamwork philosophy advocates leaders, teammates, and facilitators resolve the root cause of teamwork issues instead of making the mistake of addressing symptoms.

Though this view is discussed in many RMT materials, uncovering the root cause is heavily emphasized as a core concept in the book *Design a Right-Minded, Team-Building Workshop: 12 Steps to Create a Team That Works as One*.

Inside that book, you will find a story about a well-meaning team leader who asked me, as their team-building facilitator, if I could teach a three-day workshop in just two days. He believed a quick team event would address the problem he saw in his team.

But the problem he was seeing was only the symptom, not the root cause of the issue. Had I agreed and given him what he asked for, the team would still be struggling with the same issue. And, as a facilitator, I would have failed both the team and the leader.

Instead, by pausing to look for the root cause of the team challenge first, we ended up designing and executing a practical, Right-Minded Teamwork workshop to solve the actual underlying problem.

By seeking out the root cause first, we delivered the leader's desired result, even though the workshop we held was not what he had initially asked for.

To improve your ability to uncover root causes and read this short story, go to your favorite book retailer or RightMindedTeamwork.com and pick up your copy of *Design a Right-Minded, Team-Building Workshop: 12 Steps to Create a Team That Works as One*.

Unified Circle of Right-Minded Thinking

When your team discusses and agrees on your psychological goals – your consciously chosen set of attitudes and behaviors as described in your Work Agreements – you have created your team's collective thought system.

By uniting with each other in this way and openly committing to one another through your Work Agreements, you are renouncing Ego in yourself and your teammates and collectively committing to train your minds to follow Reason.

This process of creating team Work Agreements is your undivided declaration of interdependence. Your assertion is saying,

> *We hold these mindful truths to be self-evident that all minds are created equal, and whosoever believes that will have everlasting freedom to choose Right-Minded Teamwork.*

Your declaration plus your daily acts of living your team Work Agreements *is your return* to the forgiving Unified Circle of Right-Minded Thinking.

Work Agreements

A Work Agreement is a collective promise made by teammates to transform non-productive, adversarial behavior into collaborative teamwork behavior. Work Agreements are a key tool for teammates and teams who aspire to do no harm and work as one.

Work Agreements are not flimsy ground rules. They are emotionally mature work performance commitments. Work Agreements announce your dedication to Oneness and demonstrate your inner belief that *none of us is as smart as all of us.*

Your team's collective Work Agreements also define your team's psychological goals and thought system. They ensure you conduct your day-to-day work from within your team's Unified Circle of Right-Minded Thinking.

To learn more about the power of Work Agreements and how to use them to transform your team, go to RightMindedTeamwork.com or your favorite book retailer, and pick up your copy of **How to Facilitate Team Work Agreements**: *A Practical, 10-Step Process for Building a Right-Minded Team That Works as One.*

About the Author

The idea of "developing people and teams that work" began as a company statement for organizational consulting firm Lord & Hogan LLC, founded in 1990. Leveraging his personable but results-oriented consulting style, founder **Dan Hogan** devoted his career to transforming dysfunctional work relationships into positive, supportive bonds.

But over the course of his 40-year career, something shifted.

Through his work as an organizational development coach, performance consultant, and Certified Master Facilitator, the mission of Lord & Hogan also became Dan's own.

Better Work Relationships = Stronger, More Productive Teams

As a consultant and facilitator, Dan advocated for the individuals and managed teams he served. He emphasized the equal importance of strong team member relationships and solid business systems and processes to overall business success. His efforts spoke for themselves as his clients began to notice results.

With Dan's guidance, teams were more productive almost overnight. There were fewer day-to-day interpersonal issues. Project management efforts were finally back on track. Teams were achieving their goals.

After being stuck for so long, these teams were moving forward... smoothly. As one client said, "Dan has the unique ability to hear the confusion and bring clarity. He has helped me, our team, and our organization to move to the next level."

The Right-Minded Teamwork Model: A Legacy

Not only did Dan's efforts deliver consistent, powerful results (gaining him many long-term clients over the years) at a higher level, but his work also positively impacted the practice of behavioral change management.

Over the course of his career, Dan refined his ideas along with the help of his clients and the teams he served. Eventually, he created his own proprietary tools, processes, and strategies. Of all his models and creations, Dan's most significant accomplishment has been the development of his Right-Minded Teamwork model, which perfectly assembles all his tools and processes into a single, streamlined approach.

At its core, Right-Minded Teamwork (RMT) is a continuous improvement loop for small and large groups; it has been proven to work with teams of all sizes. No matter what team challenges or interpersonal issues are happening, RMT has the power to correct them.

By first bringing the team together under a unified set of goals, and then providing tools for teams to explore, understand, and work through their underlying concerns, Right-Minded Teamwork provides teams with the opportunity to address unproductive behaviors in a safe, non-condemning way. Focusing on acceptance, forgiveness, and self-adjustment among teammates, Right-Minded Teamwork directly addresses and resolves the root cause of even the most difficult teamwork situations.

After directly serving over 500 teams in seven countries and creating lasting tools and resources that will go on to support countless additional teams, leaders, and facilitators on every continent, Dan Hogan has left a legacy to be proud of. No longer an active facilitator, Dan has transformed his ideas and contributions into powerful, effective, team-building tools available online, providing team facilitators and team leaders around the globe access to Right-Minded Teamwork.

Books by Dan Hogan

Reason, Ego & the Right-Minded Teamwork Myth*: The Philosophy and Process for Creating a Right-Minded Team That Works Together as One*

This book explores two foundational concepts: the Right-Minded Teamwork Myth, a short tale that presents RMT's underlying teamwork philosophy, and the Right-Minded Teamwork team-building process, a step-by-step approach to implementing RMT in any team.

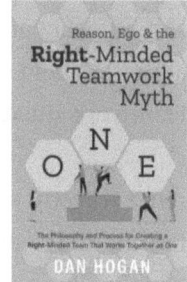

Right-Minded Teamwork in Any Team*: The Ultimate Team-Building Method to Create a Team That Works as One*

Right-Minded Teamwork is built on a framework of 5 Elements, explored in this book. These two goals and three methods are implemented into your team through three team-building workshops conducted over a six-to-12-month period. Once your team completes its third workshop, you move into a 90-day, continuous improvement operating plan that allows your team to achieve their goals, do no harm, and work together as one.

How to Facilitate Team Work Agreements: *A Practical, 10-Step Process for Building a Right-Minded Team That Works as One*

Team Work Agreements are collective pledges made by your team to transform non-productive or dysfunctional actions into positive and constructive work behavior. Though this book is written primarily for team facilitators, team leaders, and teammates may also follow these steps to create powerful, effective Work Agreements to solve and prevent interpersonal and process problems.

How to Apply the Right Choice Model: *Create a Right-Minded Team That Works as One*

The concept of Right Choice states every person has free will. Free will means you are 100% responsible for how you respond to every situation, circumstance, and event. When difficult team problems occur, you either act as an ally or an adversary. When you choose to be an ally, you demonstrate positive, accountable behavior. When you are an adversary, you behave as either a victim or a victimizer. This book and model will guide you through creating a team of productive, supportive, Right-Minded teammate allies.

7 Mindfulness Training Lessons*: Improve Teammates' Ability to Work as One with Right-Minded Thinking*

If you want your team to work together as one, you want them to think as one, too. These 7 Mindfulness Training Lessons will help you achieve a positive team mindset by guiding teammates to raise their awareness of thoughts, choices, and behaviors. Teammates may also use these lessons to create the team's Right-Minded thought system. The 7 Lessons can be summed up in one sentence, emphasizing three words: Right-Minded Teammates **accept**, **forgive**, and **adjust** their thinking and work behavior. When teammates follow these lessons, they **do no harm** while **working together as one.**

Right-Minded Teamwork*: 9 Right Choices for Building a Team That Works as One*

This quick read is an excellent Right-Minded Teamwork primer and a terrific way to introduce RMT to teammates. These nine teamwork choices are universal, self-evident, and self-validating. You want them in your team. In this book, each of the 9 Right Choices is defined, and exercises are provided for applying each choice.

Design a Right-Minded, Team-Building Workshop:
12 Steps to Create a Team That Works as One

This book includes complete instructions on how to design a practical, real-world, team-building workshop that teammates actually want to attend. Unlike many team activities labeled "team building" that are really more "team bonding," true team-building workshops are intentionally designed to solve a team's real-world problems. Written primarily for team facilitators, team leaders, and teammates may also follow these 12 steps to design an effective, transformative team workshop.

Achieve Your Organization's Strategic Plan: Create a Right-Minded Team Management System to Ensure All Teams Work as One

When a single team within an organization works together as one, they are effective and productive. When an enterprise works with the same level of synergy, it is exponentially more powerful. A Team Management System like the Right-Minded Teamwork TMS model taught in this book lays the groundwork for your organization to get every team on the same page. By following RMT's four-part rollout plan, you can create and deploy your own Team Management System, align teammate attitudes, and work behavior with company values, and bring your entire organization together to work as one and achieve your strategic plan.

The End

On behalf of **Reason** and all the **Right-Minded Teammate Decision-Makers,** we extend our best wishes to you and your teammates as you create another *Right-Minded Team that Works Together as One*.

Printed by Libri Plureos GmbH in Hamburg, Germany